FRESH DESIGNS
SHAWLS

FEATURING DESIGNS BY

Alice Twain
Anna Dalvi
Bärbel Hurst
Daniel Yuhas
Kathy Norris
Rebecca Blair
Samantha Roshak
Tabitha's Heart
Terri Bate
Theressa Silver

AND PHOTOGRAPHY BY

Robert Gladys / Fractured Photography

COOPERATIVE PRESS
Cleveland, OH
cooperativepress.com

FRESH DESIGNS: SHAWLS

Library of Congress Control Number: 2012936575
ISBN 13: 978-1-937513-04-7
First Edition
Published by Cooperative Press
http://www.cooperativepress.com

Patterns © 2012, their designers, as credited
Photos © 2012, Robert Gladys, Fractured Photography (fracturedphotography.com)

Makeup by Elle Gemma, Spell Cosmetics (spellcosmetics.com)
Models: Arabella Proffer, Elle Gemma, Rachel Harner, Susan Prahst, Terra Incognita

Every effort has been made to ensure that all the information in this book is accurate at the time of publication, however Cooperative Press neither endorses nor guarantees the content of external links referenced in this book.

If you have questions or comments about this book, or need information about licensing, custom editions, special sales, or academic/corporate purchases, please contact Cooperative Press: info@cooperativepress.com or 13000 Athens Ave C288, Lakewood, OH 44107 USA

No part of this book may be reproduced in any form, except brief excerpts for the purpose of review, without prior written permission of the publisher. Thank you for respecting our copyright.

FOR COOPERATIVE PRESS

Senior Editor: Shannon Okey
Assistant Editor: Elizabeth Green Musselman
Developmental Editor: Abra Forman
Technical Editor: Alexandra Virgiel
Production Manager: MJ Kim
With additional assistance by Sarah Jo Burch

TABLE OF CONTENTS

ALICE TWAIN	Good Luck Shawl	(page 5)
ANNA DALVI	Sea of Tulips Stole	(page 9)
BÄRBEL HURST	Tyrolean Capelet	(page 15)
DANIEL YUHAS	Shrinking Cables Shawl	(page 19)
KATHY NORRIS	Floating Cables Wrap	(page 23)
REBECCA BLAIR	Iris Shawl	(page 27)
SAMANTHA ROSHAK	Intersection Shawl	(page 33)
TABITHA'S HEART	Field of Daisies Shawl	(page 37)
TERRI BATE	Furzeleigh Lane Shawlette	(page 41)
THERESSA SILVER	Geometry Wrap	(page 47)

ACKNOWLEDGMENTS (page 50)
ABOUT COOPERATIVE PRESS AND THE FRESH DESIGNS SERIES (page 51)

GOOD LUCK SHAWL
BY ALICE TWAIN

EASY

I was moved to design a shawl that was both simple and unusual in shape: instead of the common top-down triangle I chose a half-octagon and decided to make it lacy with off-centered eyelet panels. The result is a shawl that's both extremely easy to work (nearly nothing to memorize and only a simple eyelet to knit) and rich in shape. Fool people into believing that you have become an expert knitter overnight!

I dubbed the shawl "Good Luck" because while knitting it I had a terrible sequence of misfortunes: the yarn was delayed by the Italian mail; the signed contract addressed to Cooperative Press was instead mailed by the Italian mail to Greece and therefore returned; my toilet broke so that the wall had to be partially knocked down, thus causing my closet to be dismantled and my bedroom to become unusable for several days; finally my computer totally broke as I was getting ready to mail the pattern. I am sure that all of the bad karma in this shawl was thrown upon me, and therefore now knitting it will prove very good luck for you!

SIZE
One size

FINISHED MEASUREMENTS
Wingspan 60"/152.5cm
Length 28.5"/72.5cm

MATERIALS
Waterloo Wools Kirkland Laceweight [100% merino wool; 840 yds/113g skein], color Olive & Herb; 1 skein

32-inch US #4/3.5mm circular needle

Stitch markers

GAUGE
21 sts/33 rows = 4"/10cm in stockinette stitch

PATTERN NOTES
The shawl as written uses exactly one skein of yarn with almost nothing left over. If in doubt, buy extra yarn.

PATTERN
Beginning Section
Cast on 3 sts.
Rows 1-12: Sl1 kwise, k2.
Row 13 [RS]: Sl1, k2, do not turn. *Yo, pick up and knit 1 st from side of strip, pm, pick up and knit 1 st; rep from * twice more, yo, pick up and knit 3 sts from CO edge. Turn. 16 sts.
Row 14 [WS]: Sl1, k2, purl to last 3 sts, k3.
Row 15: Sl1, k2, yo, *k to 1 st before marker, yo, k1, sl m, k1, yo; rep from * twice more, k to last 3 sts, yo, k3. 8 sts inc'd.
Row 16: Rep Row 14.
Row 17: Sl1, knit to end.
Row 18: Rep Row 14.
Rep Rows 14-18 twice more. 40 sts.

First Eyelet Sequence
Row 1 [RS] Sl1, k2, yo, *k2tog, yo, k to 1 st before marker, yo, k1, sl m, k1, yo; rep from * twice more, k2tog, yo, k to last 3 sts, k3. 8 sts inc'd.
Row 2: Sl1, k2, purl to last 3 sts, k3.
Row 3: Sl1, k2, *k2tog, yo, knit to marker, sl m, k1; rep from * twice more, k2tog, yo, k to end.
Row 4: Rep Row 2.
Rep these 4 rows twice more. 64 sts.

Second Eyelet Sequence
Row 1 [RS]: Sl1, k2, yo, *(k2tog, yo) twice, k to 1 st before marker, yo, k1, sl m, k1, yo; rep from * twice more, (k2tog, yo) twice, k to last 3 sts, yo, k3. 8 sts inc'd.
Row 2: Sl1, k2, purl to last 3 sts, k3.
Row 3: Sl1, k2, *(k2tog, yo) twice, k to marker, sl m, k1; rep from * twice more, (k2tog, yo) twice, k to end.
Row 4: Rep Row 2.
Rep these 4 rows twice more. 88 sts.

Third Eyelet Sequence
Row 1 [RS]: Sl1, k2, yo, *(k2tog, yo) 3 times, k to 1 st before marker,

yo, k1, sl m, k1, yo; rep from * twice more, (k2tog, yo) 3 times, k to last 3 sts, yo, k3. 8 sts inc'd.
Row 2: Sl1, k2, purl to last 3 sts, k3.
Row 3: Sl1, k2, *(k2tog, yo) 3 times, k to marker, sl m, k1; rep from * twice more, (k2tog, yo) 3 times, k to end.
Row 4: Rep Row 2.
Rep these 4 rows twice more. 112 sts.

Following Eyelet Sequences.
Continue to work as above, adding one more eyelet (k2tog, yo) to each sequence after every 12 rows, until you have completed a sequence of 12 rows with 10 eyelets in a row. When counting eyelets be sure not to count the increase yarn overs on either side of the markers; only count yarn overs paired with a k2tog. At this point you should have 280 sts.

Pattern Section II
Continue as above, adding another eyelet after every 8 rows, until you have completed a sequence of 8 rows with 14 eyelets in a row. 344 sts.

Pattern Section III
Continue as above, adding another eyelet after every 4 rows, until you have completed a sequence of 4 rows with 18 eyelets in a row. 376 sts.

Pattern Section IV
Row 1 [RS]: Sl1, k2, yo, *(k2tog, yo) 19 times, k to 1 st before marker, yo, k1, sl m, k1, yo; rep from * twice more, (k2tog, yo) 19 times, knit to last 3 sts, yo, k3. 384 sts.
Rows 2, 4, 6: Sl1, k2, purl to last 3 sts, k3.
Row 3: Sl1, k2, *(k2tog, yo) 20 times, k to marker, sl m, k1; rep from * twice more, (k2tog, yo) 20 times, knit to end.
Row 5: Sl1, k2, yo, *(k2tog, yo) 24 times, k to 1 st before marker, yo, k1, sl m, k1, yo; rep from * twice more, (k2tog, yo) 24 times, knit to end. 392 sts.
Row 7: Sl1, k2, *(k2tog, yo) 28 times, k to marker, sl m, k1; rep from * twice more, (k2tog, yo) 28 times, knit to end.
Row 8 [WS]: Rep Row 2.

Border
The border is worked sideways in garter stitch over 3 sts. This creates a thin, regular border that supports the eyelet rows without adding bulk and leaves the edge with ample stretch for blocking.
On LH needle, cast on an additional 3 sts.
Row 1 [RS]: K2, k2tog (1 st from border with 1 st from shawl body), turn.
Row 2 [WS]: Sl1 kwise wyif, k2.
Row 3: Sl1 kwise wyib, k1, k2tog (1 st from border with 1 st from shawl body), turn.
Rep Rows 2-3 until all shawl body stitches have been used up and only 3 sts rem on needle. Bind off.

FINISHING
Wash the shawl in warm water with a mild detergent, squeeze out as much water as possible without wringing it, lay it on a clean towel and roll it up, place the resulting "sausage" in the shower or bathtub and walk on it to remove as much water as possible. Lay the shawl on a flat surface covered with one large towel and pin it out in the shape you want. I pinned mine with only three pins in the bottom, so to produce three well-define peaks corresponding to the three increase lines, you may prefer to pin it in a half-circle shape. Leave in place until completely dry then remove all pins and weave in ends.

ABOUT ALICE TWAIN
Alice Twain started knitting and crocheting in 2004 to cope up with an extremely difficult period, and has been designing ever since. Currently she works as an editor and typesetter, and also teaches knitting workshops, translates and does technical editing on knitting patterns, and designs. In October 2011 she became part of the team behind Maglia-Uncinetto.it, an independent website on knitting and crocheting. She is one of the three founders of the Milan Stitch and Bitch group (maglia.blogspot.com). Alice Twain was born and survives in foggy Milan.

http://atknits.blogspot.com/
AliceTwain on ravelry.com

SEA OF TULIPS STOLE
BY ANNA DALVI

INTERMEDIATE

Sea of Tulips is a rectangular stole inspired by the Ottawa Tulip festival, when the town is decked out with tulips at every turn.

SIZE
Adjustable. Shown with one iteration of Chart 2.

FINISHED MEASUREMENTS
74" x 28"/188cm x 71cm

MATERIALS
Lisa Souza Cashmere Silk Fingering [55% silk, 45% cashmere; 400 yd/366m per 57g skein]; color: Garnet; 3 skeins

1 32-inch US #6/4mm circular needle

GAUGE
13 sts/26 rows = 4"/10cm in pattern (blocked)

PATTERN NOTES
This rectangular stole is worked from corner to corner. The width and length can be customized by working more or fewer repeats of certain sections of Chart 2.

PATTERN
Cast on 2 sts.
Row 1 [WS]: K2.
Row 2: Kfb twice. 4 sts.
Row 3: K4.
Begin working charts. Only RS rows are charted. Work all WS rows as: K2, purl to last 2 sts, k2.

Work Rows 1-90 of Chart 1 once.
Work Rows 1-24 of Chart 2 (from the beginning to the black line) as many times as desired. The length of the side (from the CO point to the first st on Row 23) will be the width of your rectangular stole. Each time Rows 1-24 are repeated, add 2 repeats of the center section (bordered in red on chart).

Work Rows 25-38 of Chart 2 once.
Work Rows 39-62 of Chart 2 (bordered in blue) as many times as required to reach the desired length of your stole. Measure the left side (from CO point to the last st on Row 62) to determine the length of the stole.
Work Rows 63-86 of Chart 2 as many times as you worked Rows 1-24, removing 2 repeats of the center section (bordered in red) each time the rows are repeated.
Work Rows 1-90 of Chart 3 once. 5 sts rem.

Next row [RS]: K2, k2tog, k1. 4 sts.
Next row: K2tog twice. 2 sts.
Bind off.

FINISHING
Sew in ends and block as a rectangle.

ABOUT ANNA DALVI
Anna is originally from the west coast of Sweden, but has traded the rugged cliffs of Bohuslän for the Canadian wilderness. In her knitting, Anna enjoys variety more than anything else – from intricate lace to sprawling cables, and differences in color and texture.

http://www.knitandknag.com
knitandknag on ravelry.com

CHART 1 (LEFT)

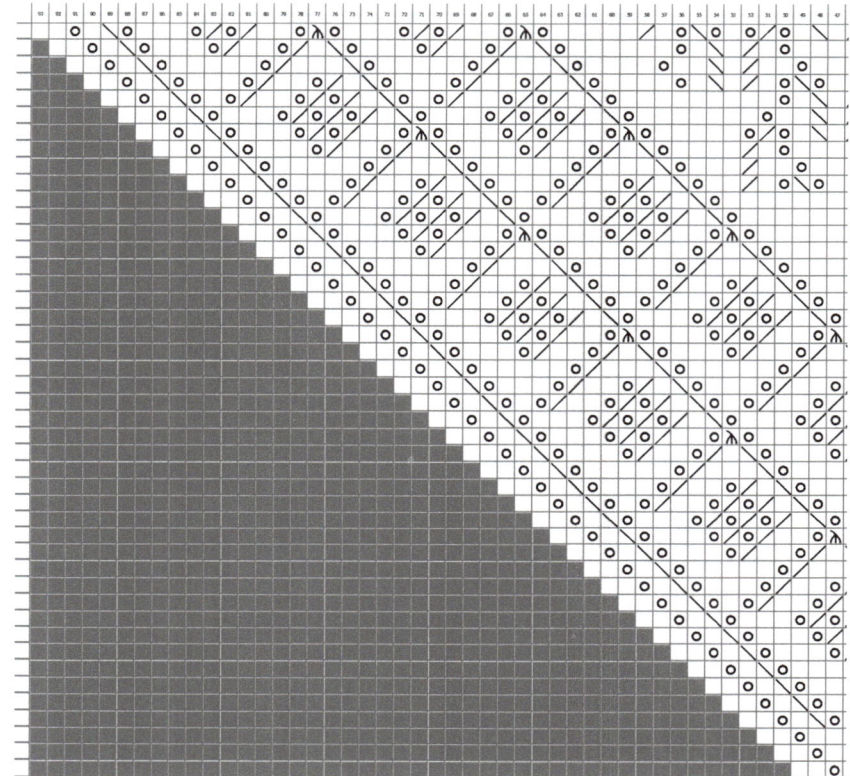

CHART 2 (LEFT)

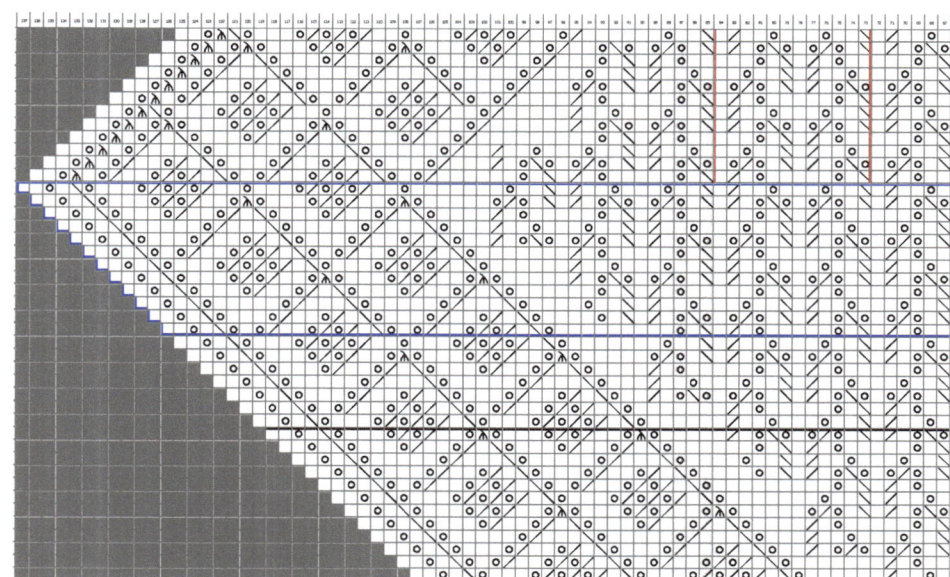

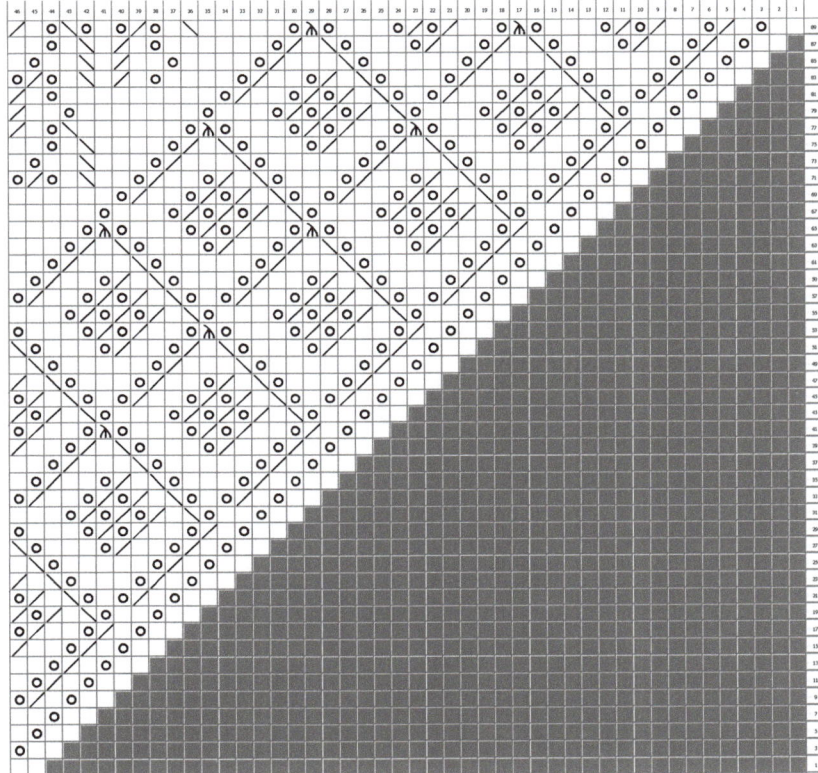

CHART 1 (RIGHT)

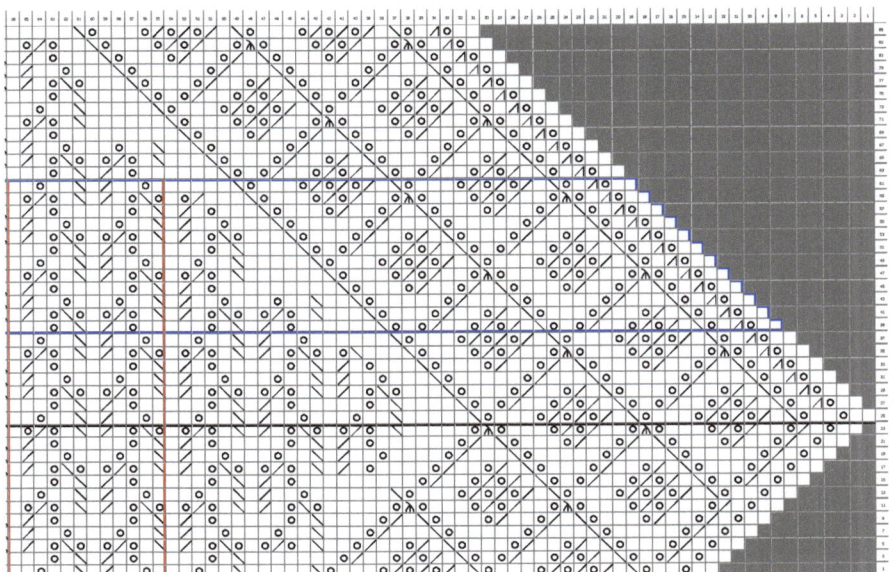

CHART 2 (RIGHT)

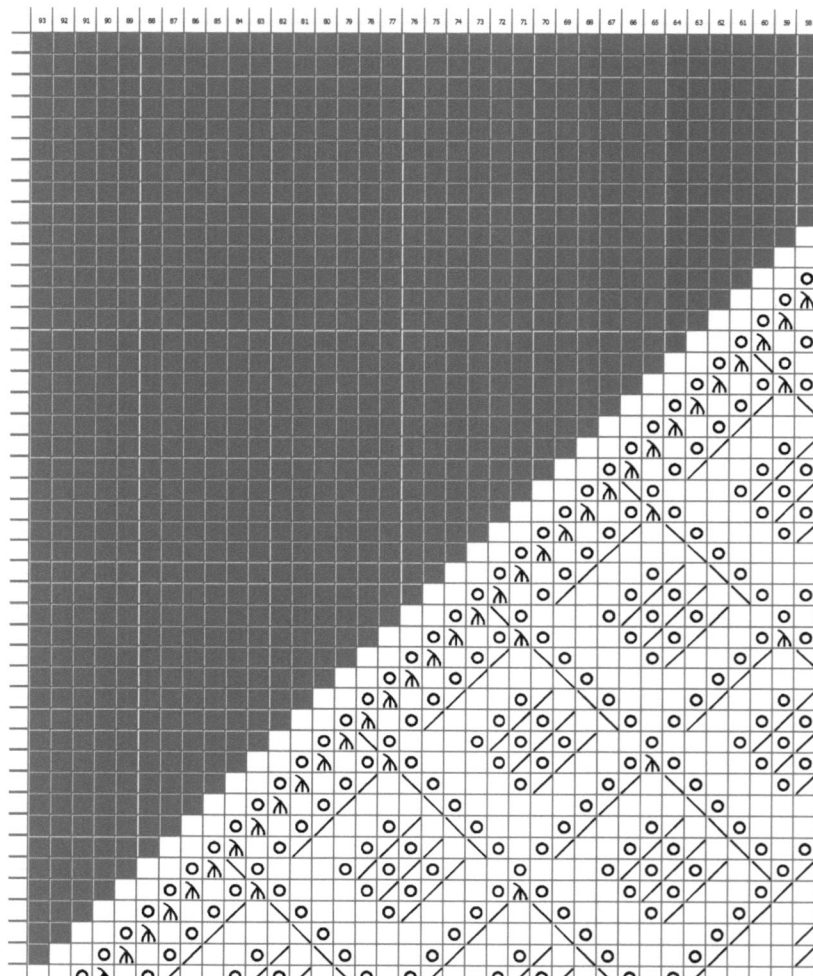

CHART 3 (LEFT)

Legend:

□ **knit** — knit stitch

⊙ **yo** — Yarn Over

◩ **k3tog** — Knit three stitches together as one

◪ **ssk** — Slip one stitch as if to knit, Slip another stitch as if to knit. Insert left-hand needle into front of these 2 stitches and knit them together

◪ **k2tog** — Knit two stitches together as one stitch

⋏ **sl1 k2tog psso** — slip 1, k2tog, pass slip stitch over k2tog

■ **No Stitch** — Placeholder - No stitch made.

⬠ **k5tog** — Knit five stitches together as one

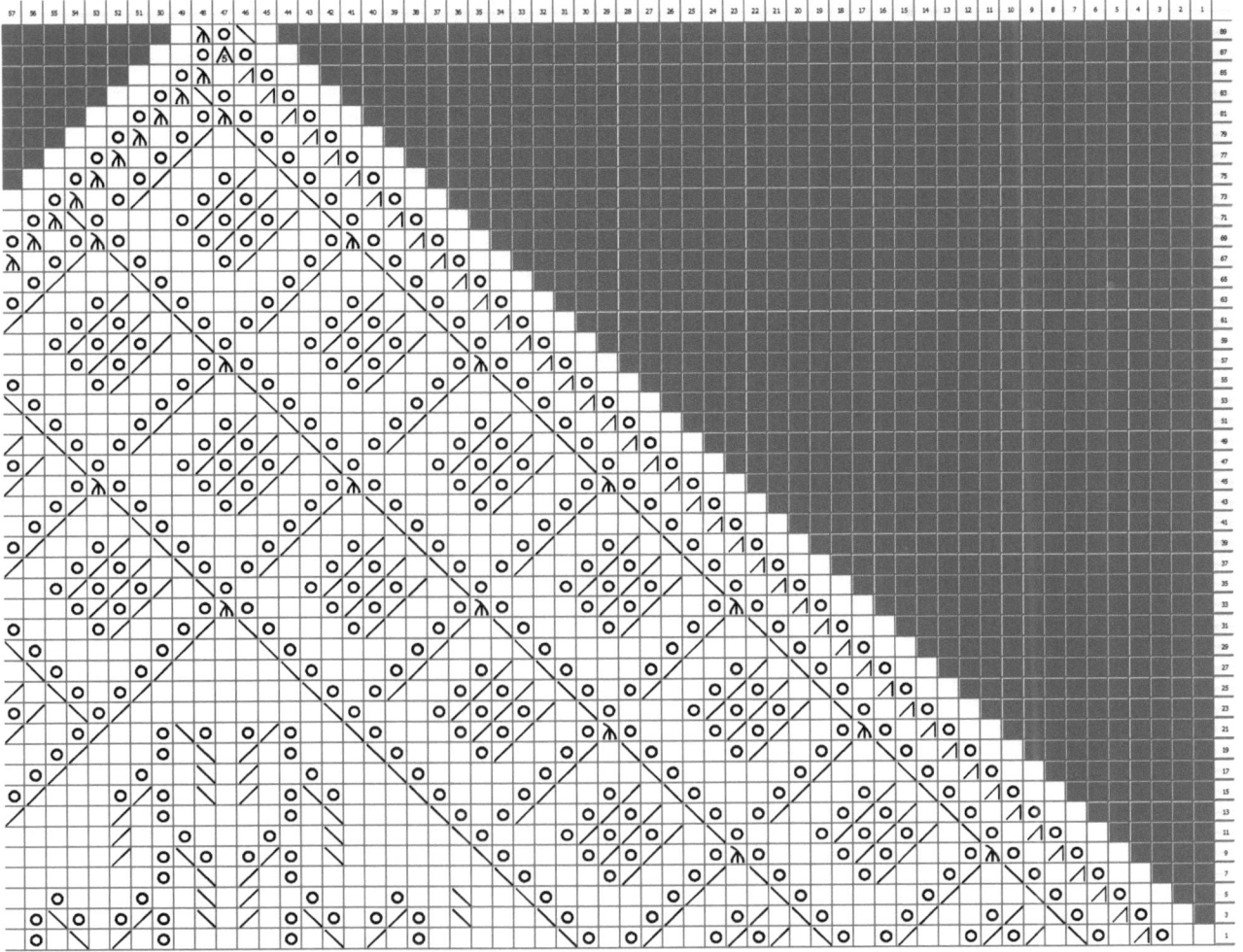

CHART 3 (RIGHT)

TYROLEAN CAPELET
BY BÄRBEL HURST

INTERMEDIATE

My projects usually are inspired by vintage style – so this capelet shows traditional patterns with fresh colors inspired by the patterns of the 1940s – cables, and some embroidered flowers.

SIZE
One size

FINISHED MEASUREMENTS
Bottom circumference 70"/178cm
13"/33cm high at center back

MATERIALS
The Sanguine Gryphon Free Range [100% organic wool; 285 yds/260m per 113g skein]; color: Fayoumi; 2 skeins.

1 32-inch US #6/4mm circular needle

Stitch markers
Cable needle (cn)
Embroidery floss and needle

GAUGE
23 sts/28 rows = 4"/10cm in stockinette

PATTERN NOTES
Shawl is knitted from the top down in five wedge-shaped sections.

Only RS rows are shown on charts. On WS rows, always work sts as they appear (knit the knits and purl the purls).

PATTERN
Cast on 66 sts. Knit 1 row.
Set-up row [WS]: (K1, pm, k10, pm) twice, k1, pm, k20, pm, k1, (pm, k10, pm, k1) twice.

Row 1 [RS]: K1, sl m, work Chart 1 beg at red line and ending at last st, sl m, k1, sl m, work Chart 1 beg at first st and ending at last st, sl m, k1, sl m, work Chart 2, sl m, k1, sl m, work Chart 1 beg at first st and ending at last st, sl m, k1, sl m, work Chart 1 beg at first st and ending at blue line, sl m, k1.
Row 2 [WS]: Work sts as they appear.

Continue as set by Rows 1-2 until all 75 rows of charts are complete, ending with a RS row. 274 sts.
Next row [WS]: Purl.
Next row [RS]: K1, purl to last st, k1.
Rep the last 2 rows once more.
BO all sts purlwise.

FINISHING
Beg at lower right corner, with RS facing, pick up and knit 2 sts for every 3 rows up right front edge, 1 st in every CO st around neck, and 2 sts for every 3 rows down left front edge. Knit 3 rows. BO loosely. Block.

Using the photos for reference, embroider flowers, stems, and leaves, using Lazy Daisy stitches and French knots.

ABOUT BÄRBEL HURST
Bärbel lives in Berlin, Germany with her family. She has a degree in historical sciences and a deep affection for fashion history. She works as an indie designer and loves to collect beautiful vintage garments.

http://www.emmasommerfeld.de/
EmmaSommerfeld on ravelry.com

CHART 1

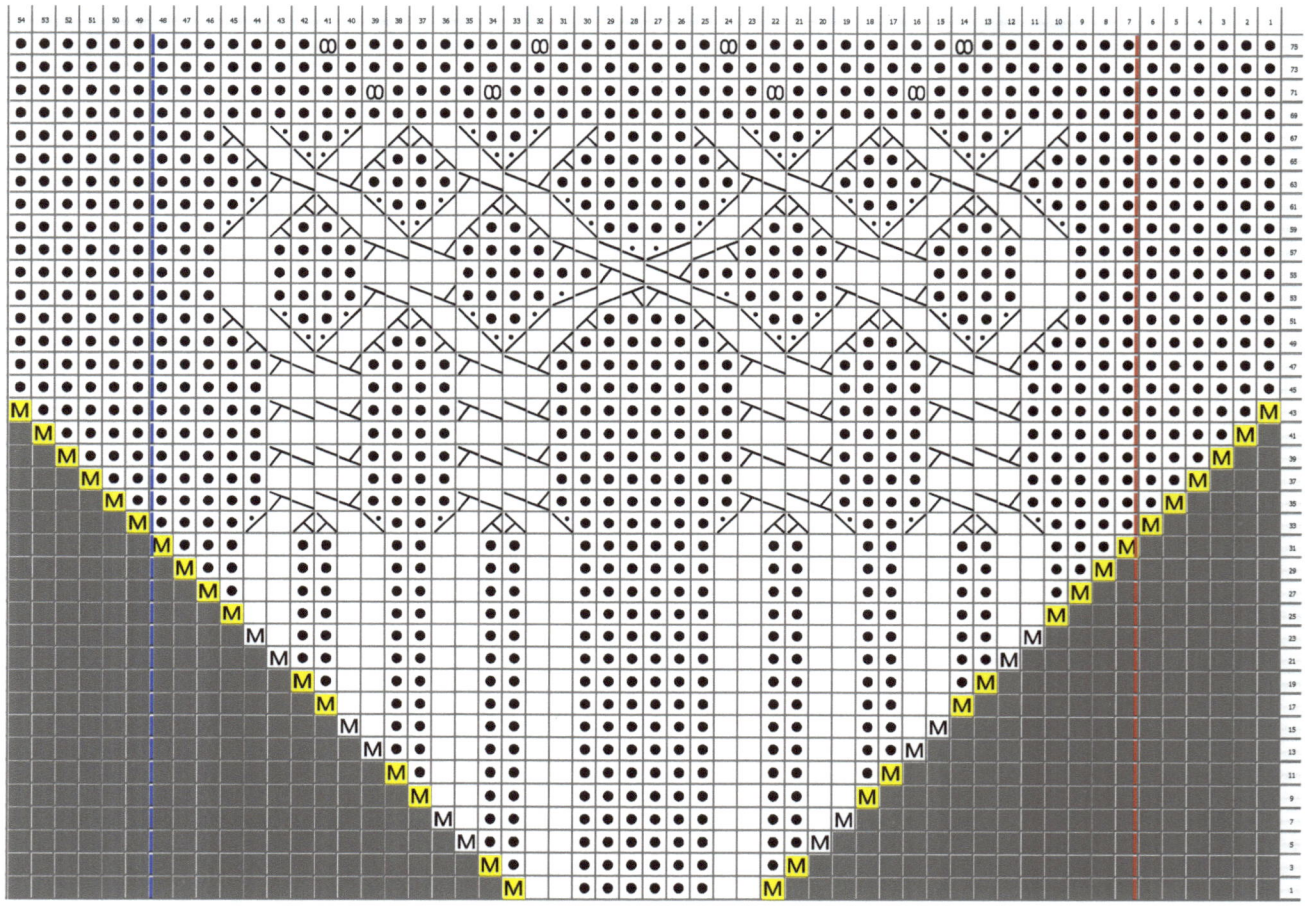

Legend:

	No Stitch
▨	Placeholder - No stitch made.

	make 1 purl
M	With LH ndl, lift strand between ndls from back to front. Purl this loop.

	knit
☐	knit stitch

	purl
•	purl stitch

	make one
M	Make one by lifting strand in between stitch just worked and the next stitch, knit into back of this thread.

CHART 2

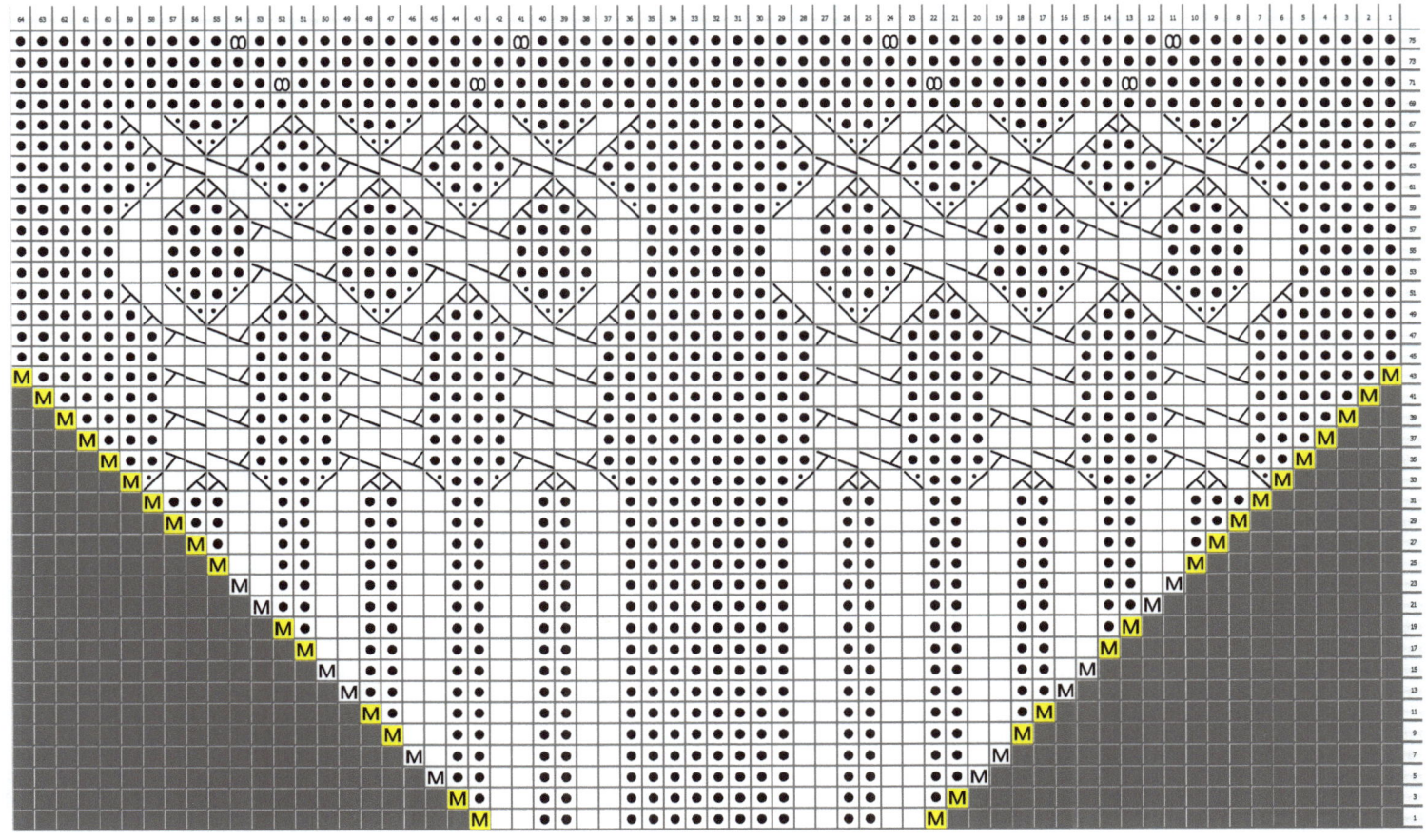

	c2 over 1 left P
	sl2 to CN, hold in front. p1, k2 from CN

	c2 over 1 right P
	sl1 to CN, hold in back. k2, p1 from CN

	c2 over 2 left
	sl 2 to CN, hold in front. k2, k2 from CN

	c2 over 2 left P
	sl 2 to CN, hold in front. p2, k2 from CN

	c2 over 2 right P
	sl2 to CN, hold in back. k2, p2 from CN

	nupp
	(k1 p1 k1 p1 k1) in stitch, take first 4 stitches created over the last

SHRINKING CABLES SHAWL

BY DANIEL YUHAS

INTERMEDIATE

This simple shawl is worked from the bottom up with cables that shrink each time they cross. The garment shaping is incorporated into the cable pattern, and the fabric gets skinnier as you progress, so the knitting goes faster and faster as you near the end.

SIZE
One size

FINISHED MEASUREMENTS
An arc-shaped shawl, 52"/132cm at bottom, narrowing to 24"/51cm; 20"/51cm long

MATERIALS
Karabella Soft Tweed [100% wool; 108yd/98m per 50g skein; color: 1080 (light grey); 5 skeins

1 36-inch US #7/4.5mm circular needle

Cable needle (cn)

GAUGE
18 sts/26 rows = 4"/10cm in stockinette stitch

PATTERN NOTES
This shawl is worked from the bottom up. All shaping is incorporated into the cable pattern. Beginning with the second cable crossing, each cable decreases by one stitch as it crosses. As each cable column tapers down from ten stitches to three, the shawl forms a gentle arc shape.

"Work n rows even" means to continue working the 5 selvage sts at each end as established in the first two rows, while working the sts in between as they appear--knit the knits and purl the purls.

PATTERN
Cast on 218 sts.
Row 1 [RS]: Sl1, p1, k3, (k10, p1) 18 times, k10, k3, p1, k1.
Row 2 [WS]: Sl1, p1, k3, (p10, k1) 18 times, p10, k3, p2.
Work 8 rows even.

Row 11: Sl1, p1, k3, (sl 5 sts to cn and hold to front, k5, k5 from cn, p1, k10, p1) 9 times, sl 5 to cn and hold to front, k5, k5 from cn, k3, p1, k1.
Work 9 rows even.

Row 21: Sl1, p1, k3, (k10, p1, sl 5 sts to cn and hold to back, k5, k2tog from cn, k3 from cn, p1) 9 times, k10, k3, p1, k1. 209 sts.
Work 9 rows even.

Row 31: Sl1, p1, k3, (sl 5 sts to cn and hold to front, k3, ssk, k5 from cn, p1, k9, p1) 9 times, sl 5 to cn and hold to front, k3, ssk, k5 from cn, k3, p1, k1. 199 sts.
Work 9 rows even.

Row 41: Sl1, p1, k3, (k9, p1, sl 5 sts to cn and hold to back, k4, k2tog from cn, k3 from cn, p1) 9 times, k9, k3, p1, k1. 190 sts.
Work 7 rows even.

Row 49: Sl1, p1, k3, (sl 4 sts to cn and hold to front, k3, ssk, k4 from cn, p1, k8, p1) 9 times, sl 4 sts to cn and hold to front, k3, ssk, k4 from cn, k3, p1, k1. 180 sts.
Work 7 rows even.

Row 57: Sl1, p1, k3, (k8, p1, sl 4 sts to cn and hold to back, k3, k2tog from cn, k2 from cn, p1) 9 times, k8, k3, p1, k1. 171 sts.
Work 7 rows even.

Row 65: Sl1, p1, k3, (sl 4 sts to cn and hold to front, k2, ssk, k4 from cn, p1, k7, p1) 9 times, sl 4 sts to cn and hold to front, k2, ssk, k4 from cn, k3, p1, k1. 161 sts.
Work 7 rows even.

Row 73: Sl1, p1, k3, (k7, p1, sl 4 to cn and hold to back, k3, k2tog from cn, k2 from cn, p1) 9 times, k7, k3, p1, k1. 152 sts.
Work 5 rows even.

Row 79: Sl1, p1, k3, (sl 3 to cn and hold to front, k2, ssk, k3 from cn, p1, k6, p1) 9 times, sl 3 to cn and hold to front, k2, ssk, k3 from cn, k3, p1, k1. 142 sts.
Work 5 rows even.

Row 85: Sl1, p1, k3, (k6, p1, sl 3 to cn and hold to back, k3, k2tog from cn, k1 from cn, p1) 9 times, k6, k3, p1, k1. 133 sts.
Work 5 rows even.

Row 91: Sl1, p1, k3, (sl 3 sts to cn and hold to front, k1, ssk, k3 from cn, p1, k5, p1) 9 times, sl 3 to cn and hold to front, k1, ssk, k3 from cn, k3, p1, k1. 123 sts.
Work 5 rows even.

Row 97: Sl1, p1, k3, (k5, p1, sl 3 sts to cn and hold to back, k2, k2tog from cn, k1 from cn, p1) 9 times, k5, k3, p1, k1. 114 sts.
Work 3 rows even.

Row 101: Sl1, p1, k3, (sl 2 to cn and hold to front, k1, ssk, k2 from cn, p1, k4, p1) 9 times, sl 2 to cn and hold to front, k1, ssk, k2 from cn, k3, p1, k1.
104 sts.
Work 3 rows even.

Row 105: Sl1, p1, k3, (k4, p1, sl 2 to cn and hold to back, k2, k2tog from cn, p1) 9 times, k4, k3, p1, k1. 95 sts.
Work 3 rows even.

Row 109: Sl1, p1, k3, (sl 2 to cn and hold to front, ssk, k2 from cn, p1, k3, p1) 9 times, sl 2 to cn and hold to front, ssk, k2 from cn, k3, p1, k1. 85 sts.
Row 110 [WS]: Sl1, p1, k3, *p3, k1; rep from * to last 8 sts, p3, k3, p2.
Row 111: Sl1, p1, k3, *k3, p1; rep from * to last 8 sts, k6, p1, k1.
Row 112: Rep Row 110.
Row 113: Rep Row 111.
Row 114: Sl1, purl to end.
Bind off all sts.

FINISHING
Weave in ends. Gently wet block.

ABOUT DANIEL YUHAS
I taught myself to knit during a break at college, fumbling over the illustrations in a teach-yourself book, and the obsession just keeps getting deeper as the years go by. My designs have appeared in books and magazines, and I've taught knitters new tricks at festivals and on the subway. It's pretty amazing how you can make just about anything you want with two sticks, some string, and two simple stitches.

http://www.superfunknits.com
moltingyeti on ravelry.com

FLOATING CABLES WRAP

BY KATHY NORRIS

INTERMEDIATE

Elfin cables float on a mesh fabric making this wrap light and airy, perfect for balmy breezes. Beads emphasize the cables and add a bit of weight along the bottom edge.

SIZE
One size

FINISHED MEASUREMENTS
72" x 20.5"/183cm x 52cm

MATERIALS
Pigeonroof Studios 80/20 Laceweight [80% merino wool; 20% tussah silk; 1000 yd/914 m per 100g skein]; color: Juniper; 1 skein

1 40-inch US #4/3.5mm circular needle

Seed beads size 8/0, 1040 (approximately 40 grams)
Collapsible bead needle or dental floss threader to string beads onto yarn
Cable needle (cn)
Crochet hook US #11/1.10mm or size to work hook bead knitting
11 stitch markers to mark end of each pattern repeat (optional)

GAUGE
25 sts/24 rows = 4"/10cm over pattern stitch, blocked

PATTERN NOTES
String 390 beads before casting on. One bead will be placed between each purl stitch on Row 1, by sliding bead against stitch on RH needle before purling the next stitch.

HB (hook bead knitting): Knit the stitch where bead is to be placed. Pick up bead with crochet hook and take the stitch off the needle with the crochet hook (crochet hook will have bead above stitch on hook). Pull the stitch through the bead. Place the stitch back onto the right needle.

PATTERN
String 390 beads before casting on, sliding the beads down the length of the yarn so that you have enough yarn for cast on.

Beg at bottom of wrap, cast on 392 sts.

Set-up rows:
Row 1 [RS]: K1, *p1, slide bead up between sts; rep from * to last st, k1.
Row 2: Purl.
Row 3: *K1, (yo, ssk) 4 times, (k2tog, yo) 4 times, k1, (yo, ssk) 4 times, (k2tog, yo) 4 times; rep from * 10 times more; k1, (yo, ssk) 4 times, (k2tog, yo) 4 times, k1.
Row 4: Purl.

Work Rows 1-32 of Chart 3 times, then Rows 1-16 once. Note that only RS rows are shown on chart. Purl all WS rows.

Bind off all sts as foll: K1, *k1, transfer 2 sts back to LH needle, k2tog tbl; rep from * to end.

FINISHING
Block so that scalloped edges along bottom and top edge of wrap come to a point. Weave in ends.

ABOUT KATHY NORRIS
Kathy has had a love affair with fiber arts for as long as she can remember. Her knitting designs can be found in various books and magazines. She lives with her husband, daughter, and 3 fur-children in Oklahoma.

http://www.kathynorrisdesigns.com/
knittingmuse on ravelry.com

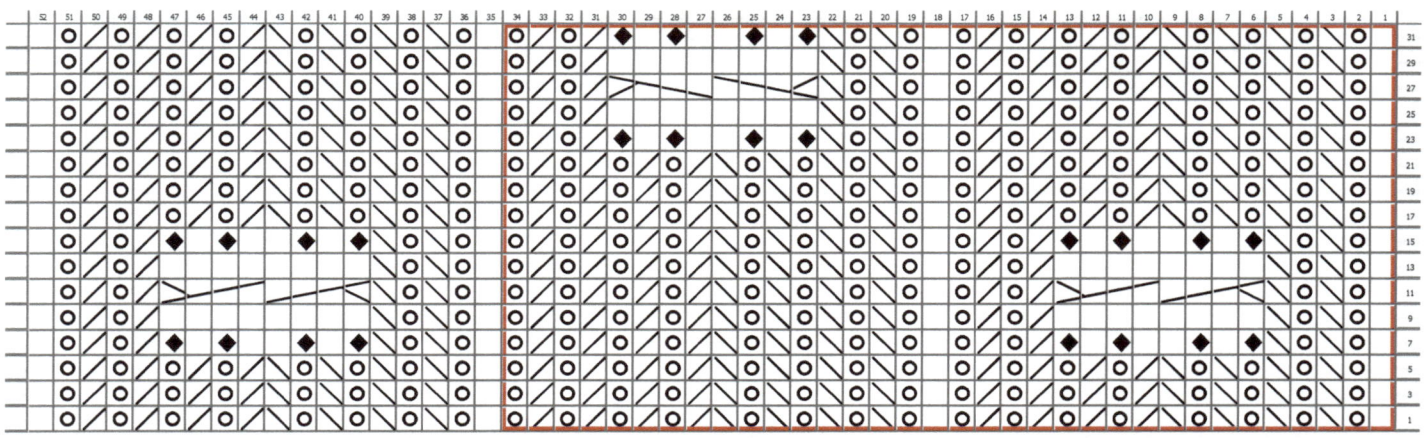

Legend:

	knit
□	knit stitch

	yo
⊙	Yarn Over

	ssk
◧	Slip one stitch as if to knit, Slip another stitch as if to knit. Insert left-hand needle into front of these 2 stitches and knit them together

	k2tog
◩	Knit two stitches together as one stitch

	hook bead knit
◆	K st where bead is to be placed. Pick up bead with crochet hk and take the stitch off the ndl with the hk (hk will have bead above st on hk). Pull the st through the bead. Place the st back onto the RH ndl.

	c4 over 4 right
	sl4 to CN, hold in back. k4, then k4 from CN

	c4 over 4 left
	sl4 to CN, hold in front. k4, k4 from CN

IRIS SHAWL
BY REBECCA BLAIR

EXPERIENCED

Iris looks like a traditional Shetland stole, but it's put together in the Orenburg lace style: knitted in one piece from end to end, with the edging knit simultaneously with the central pattern. This minimizes the amount of finishing work left to do when the knitting is completed, and lets the patterns flow smoothly and naturally into one another.

The shawl is named for the way the motifs enclosed in diamonds look like eyes, some open and some closed.

SIZE
One size

FINISHED MEASUREMENTS
82" x 22"/56cm x 208.5cm

MATERIALS
A Verb for Keeping Warm Holding [100% superfine alpaca; 1085 yards per 3.5oz skein]; color: The Peacock's Wild Plume; 1 skein

1 32-inch US #3/3.25mm circular needle

Waste yarn
Stitch markers

GAUGE
28 sts/36 rows = 4" in garter stitch, after blocking
24 sts/32 rows = 4" in center pattern, after blocking

PATTERN NOTES
This stole is knitted in one piece. It begins with a narrow strip of edging from which stitches are picked up for the body of the stole, and ends with another strip of edging attached as it is worked. Edging is worked on either side of the main body section for the length of the stole, and is set off by stitch markers.

The corners of the shawl are mitered using short rows, so that the edging there lies flat without puckering. When knitting a stitch that has been wrapped on a previous row, knit the stitch together with its wrap to prevent holes. Where a stitch has been wrapped twice, knit it together with both of its wraps.

This stole is worked in garter stitch lace: knit every row, and all decreases are either k2tog, k3tog, or k3tog tbl. The charts are to be read literally—they do not show the work as it appears from the right side, like other charts.

PATTERN
Cast on 7 sts using a provisional method. K 1 row.

Begin following Chart 1 (Edging). Work according to Chart until nine 20-row repeats have been completed.

Work Chart 2 (First Corner) until all 10 rows have been completed. Do not turn.

With free end of needle, pick up each bar between garter ridges along the straight edge of the edging strip. 90 sts picked up. Place marker to divide edging from body and k across. Do not turn. Place another marker.

Carefully undo provisional cast on, slipping sts onto free needle as they become live. 7 sts. Work Chart 3 (Second Corner) over these sts. Do not turn after corner chart is completed. Slip marker. (K4, kfb, k5) 9 times. 99 sts between markers. Slip marker. Work Row 11 of Edging.

From now on, work Edging patt as established on either side of the main body sts, set off by the stitch markers.

Next row: Work Row 12 of Edging, sl m, work Row 1 of Chart 4 (Border), sl m, work Row 11 of Edging.

Continue to work Border flanked by Edging on both sides until 6 repeats of Border rows 2-38 have been worked.

Work Chart 5 (Center Set-Up) flanked by Edging.

Work Chart 6 (Center) flanked by Edging until 6 repeats of Center have been worked.

Work Chart 7 (Border Set-Up) flanked by Edging. Beginning with Row 2, work Chart 4 (Border) flanked by Edging until 6 repeats of Border rows 2-38 have been worked.

Next row: Work Row 10 of Edging, slip marker, (k4, k2tog, k5) 9 times. 90 sts remain in central section. Work Row 9 of Edging.

Work Chart 8 (Third Corner) until all chart rows have been completed. Remove marker that divides edging from body on this side. Turn work.

Next row: Work Row 1 of Edging.
Next row: Work Row 2 of Edging, knitting the last edging st tog with the first st from the central section. Turn.
Next row: Work Row 3 of edging.

Continue working Edging, attaching it to the central section at the end of every even-numbered row, until all sts from central section have been consumed and only edging sts remain. Do not turn, and leave marker in place. Work Chart 9 (Fourth Corner) Row 1 over the sts that remain on the left needle. Continue to work Fourth Corner until all chart rows are completed. Remove marker. 7 sts remain on each needle. Break yarn.

Graft the two sets of sts together in garter stitch as foll:
Slip the first st on the right needle to the left needle. *Insert right needle purlwise through the first st on the left needle, then knitwise into the second st. Pull the second st through the first, dropping the first st off the needle and transferring the second st to the right needle. Insert left needle through the first st on the right needle and then into the second. Pull the second st through the first, dropping the first st off the needle and transferring the second st to the left needle.* Repeat from * to * until all sts have been drawn through. 1 st remains.

Cut a short length of yarn and thread it through remaining st. Tie half a square knot to secure.

FINISHING
Weave in all ends, but don't cut them off yet. Block the shawl by soaking in lukewarm water, squeezing out excess water in a towel, and laying flat to dry. Pin out each point in the edging, stretching the shawl taut. When shawl is completely dry, unpin it and cut off the woven-in ends.

ABOUT REBECCA BLAIR
Rebecca lives and knits in southern Ontario. Her favorite projects are elaborate old-fashioned lace shawls and doilies, or warm winter accessories.

http://doiliesarestylish.blogspot.com
bewilderbeast on ravelry.com

CHART 1

Legend:

	knit
	knit stitch
o	**yo**
	Yarn Over
/	**k2tog**
	Knit two stitches together as one stitch
■	**No Stitch**
	Placeholder - No stitch made.
A	**wrap and turn**
\	**ssk**
	Slip one stitch as if to knit, Slip another stitch as if to knit. Insert left-hand needle into front of these 2 stitches and knit them together
N	**k3tog tbl**
	Knit three stitches together through back loops
⋀	**sl1 k2tog psso**
	slip 1, k2tog, pass slip stitch over k2tog
⟋	**k3tog**
	Knit three stitches together as one

CHART 2 - FIRST

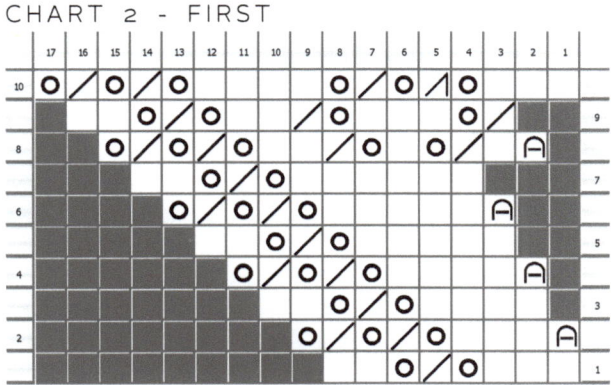

CHART 3 - SECOND

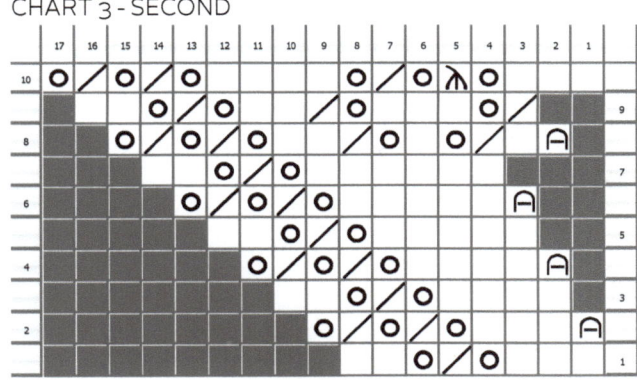

CHART 4 - BORDER

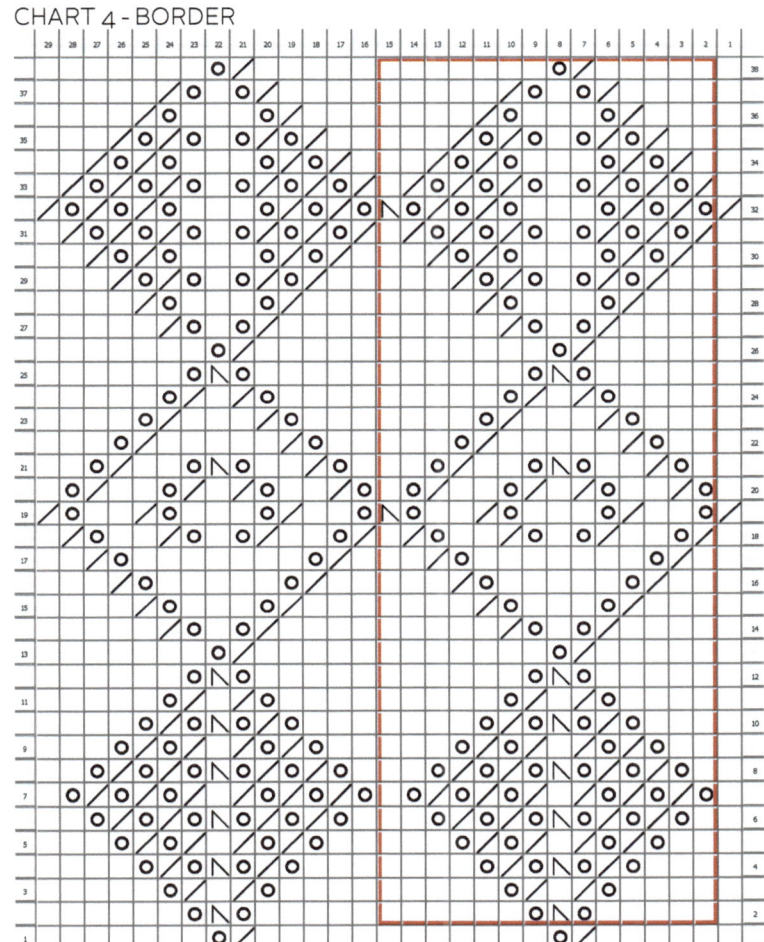

CHART 5 - CENTER

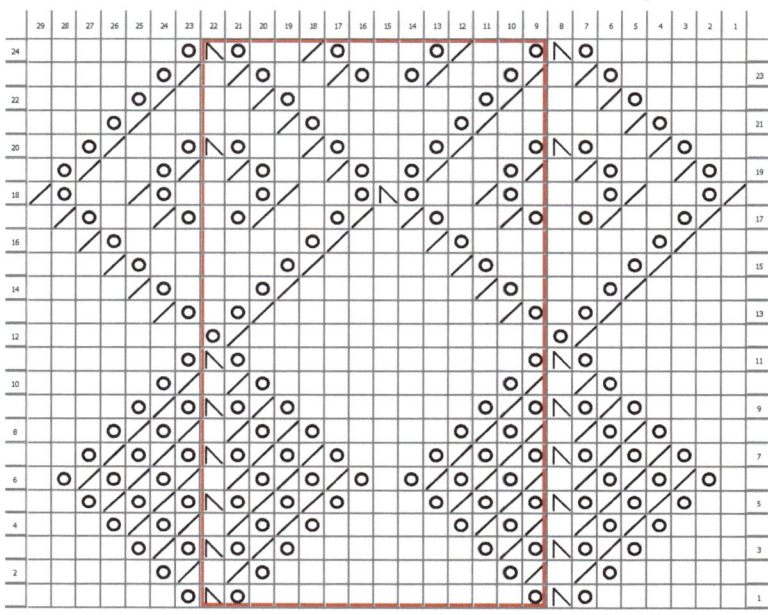

CHART 6 - CENTER

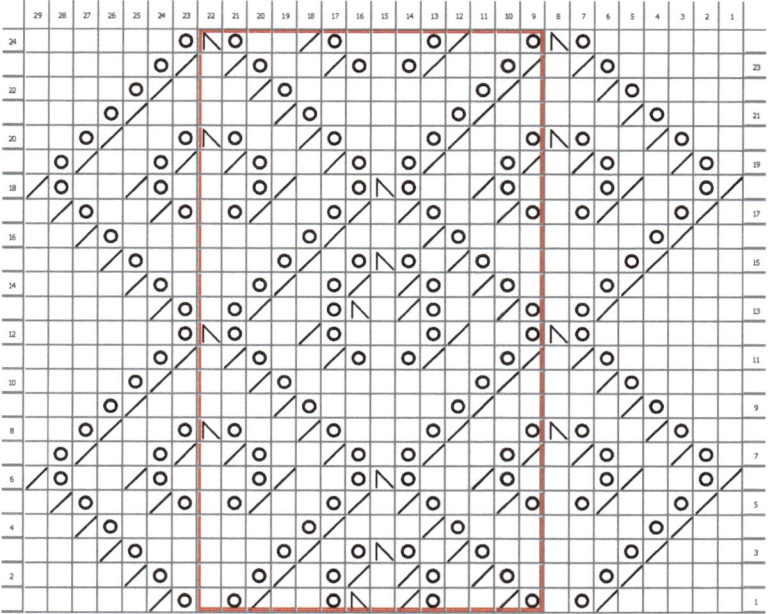

CHART 7 - BORDER

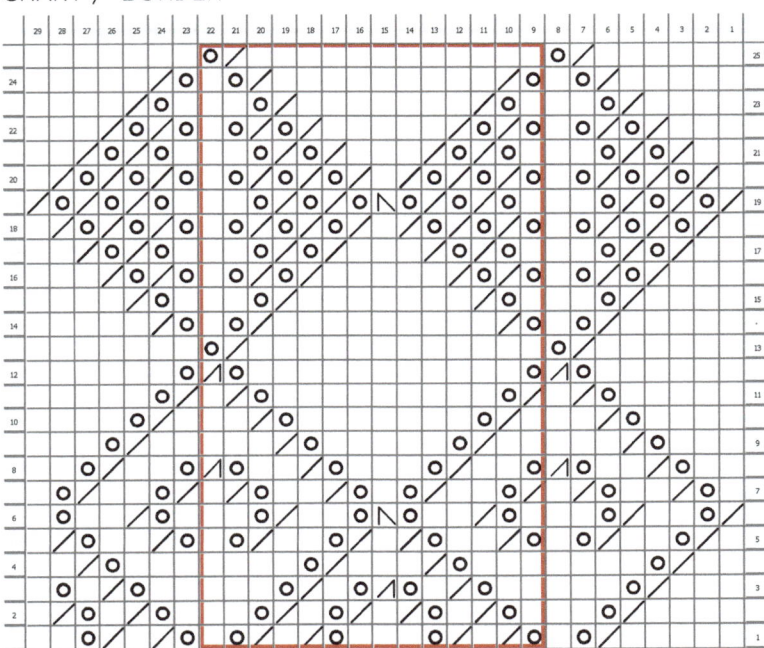

CHART 8 - THIRD

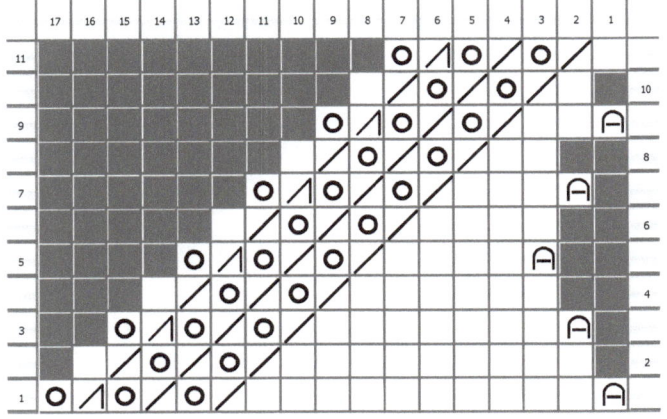

CHART 9 - FOURTH

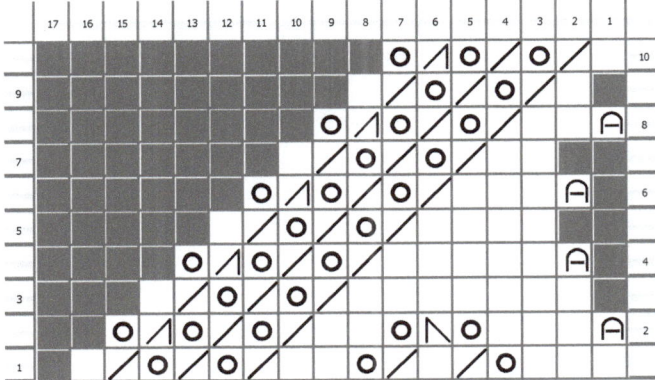

INTERSECTION SHAWL

BY SAMANTHA ROSHAK

INTERMEDIATE

I love to knit lace, but wearing it can be another story. Frilly, girly and delicate things don't fit my life or my personality. I like to wear cozy, casual and capable pieces. For this shawl I was determined to combine my knitting passion and my wardrobe needs. To find, in effect their intersection.

I used short row construction to create a rounded, shape flattering edge with a ribbed border for stability, weight and interest. The beautiful and simple lace pattern covers your back without interruption, while the off-set ribbing frames the lace and give the shawl a flat edge.

SIZE
One size

FINISHED MEASUREMENTS
Wingspan 67"/170cm
Length at center back 21"/53.5cm

MATERIALS
Blue Moon Fiber Arts BFL Sport [100% Bluefaced Leicester wool; 661 yds/604 m per 226 g skein]; color: Raspberry Mousse; 1 skein.

1 32-inch or longer US #5/3.75mm circular needle, or size needed to obtain gauge
1 12-inch or longer US #6/4mm circular needle or 1 size larger than smaller needle (for bind off only)

Cable needle (cn)

GAUGE
13 sts/28 rows = 4"/10cm in lace pattern, blocked

PATTERN NOTES
The first stitch of all short rows is slipped. This makes the stitch a tiny bit smaller, to help prevent holes, and turns the stitch sideways so it is easier to see and feel the gaps.

The yarn used in this shawl is light and lofty. For best results when substituting yarn, choose one with similar characteristics.

C2/3L: sl 1 to cn, hold in front, kfb, k1 from cn
C2/3R: sl 1 to cn, hold in back, kfb, k1 from cn
C3/4L: sl 2 to cn, hold in front, kfb, k2 from cn
C3/4R: sl 2 to cn, hold in back, kfb, k2 from cn
Cgr: close gap right. Pick up the right leg of st below the first st on the left needle from back to front (it's the st below the slipped stitch) with the right needle, slip the st to the left needle and knit tbl. This technique is very much like a lifted inc. The final st will be twisted.
Cgl: close gap left. Pick up the left leg of st two below the last st on the right needle from back to front (it's in the same column as the first st on the left needle) and knit it. This technique is very much like a lifted inc. The final st will be twisted.
LT: left twist. sl 1 to cn and hold to the front, k1, k1 from cn.
RT: right twist. sl 1 to cn and hold to the back, k1, k1 from cn.

Both written-out and charted instructions are provided for this shawl.

PATTERN
With smaller needles cast on 180 sts. Knit 3 rows.

Body (Chart 1)
The body section is a series of short rows. Each row decreases the working sts by one. Once the short rows begin, the first st of all subsequent rows is slipped, kwise wyib on RS rows and pwise wyif on WS rows. This turns the st to the side (making both legs of the slipped st parallel) and makes the space between gaps a tiny bit smaller. It helps prevent holes and makes it easier to see and feel the gaps as you work.

Row 1 [RS]: P2, *p1, k1, p4, k1, p1; rep from * to last 2 sts, p2.
Row 2 [WS]: K2, *k1, p1, k4, p1, k1; rep from * to last 2 sts, k1, turn.
Row 3: Sl1, *p1, yo, ssk, p2, k2tog, yo, p1; rep from * to last 2 sts, p1, turn.
Row 4: Sl1, *k1, p2, k2, p2, k1; rep from * to last 2 sts before the gap, k1, turn.
Row 5: Sl1, p1, yo, ssk, k2tog, yo, p2, *p2, yo, ssk, k2tog, yo, p2; rep

from * to last st before the gap, turn.
Row 6: Sl1, k1, p4, k2, *k2, p4, k2; rep from * to last 7 sts before the gap, k2, p4, k1, turn.
Row 7: Sl1, k1, LT, k1, p2, *p2, k1, LT, k1, p2; rep from * to last 8 sts before the gap, p2, k1, LT, k1, p1, turn.
Row 8: Sl1, p4, k2, *k2, p4, k2; rep from * to last 7 sts before the gap, k2, p3, k1, turn.
Row 9: Sl1, p2, k1, p2, (p2, k1, p2, k1, p2) rep to last 7 sts before the gap, p2, k1, p3, turn.
Row 10: Sl1, k2, p1, k2, *k2, p1, k2, p1, k2; rep from * to last 6 sts before the gap, k2, p1, k2, turn.
Row 11: Sl1, p1, yo, ssk, p1, *p1, k2tog, yo, p2, yo, ssk, p1; rep from * to last 6 sts before the gap, p1, k2tog, yo, p2, turn.
Row 12: Sl1, k1, p2, k1, *k1, p2, k2, p2, k1; rep from * to last 5 sts before the gap, k1, p2, k1, turn.
Row 13: Sl1, p1, yo, ssk, *k2tog, yo, p4, yo, ssk; rep from * to last 5 sts before the gap, k2tog, yo, p2, turn.
Row 14: Sl1, k1, p2, *p2, k4, p2; rep from * to last 4 sts before the gap, p2, k1, turn.
Row 15: Sl1, k1, *RT, k1, p4, k1; rep from * to last 5 sts before the gap, RT, k1, p1, turn. Note: the rep for this row is shifted one st to the right to accommodate the cable.
Row 16: Sl1, k1, p1, *p2, k4, p2; rep from * to last 3 sts before the gap, p1, k1, turn.
Row 17: Sl1, p1, *p1, k1, p4, k1, p1; rep from * to last 3 sts before the gap, p2, turn.
Row 18: Sl1, k1, *k1, p1, k4, p1, k1; rep from * to last 2 sts before the gap, k1, turn.
Row 19: Sl1, *p1, yo, ssk, p2, k2tog, yo, p1; rep from * to last 2 sts before the gap, p1, turn.
Rep Rows 4-19 until there are 62 working sts, with 59 sts on each side separated by gaps. End with Row 7.

Close gaps
Cut working yarn, leaving a tail to weave in. Slip all remaining sts to right needle. Begin working with the RS facing you.

Pick up and k2 sts along the edge of the first 3 rows, *k1, cgr; rep from * until all gaps to the right of the working sts are closed (your tail will be here), k to next gap (62 sts), *cgl, k1; rep from * to end of row, pick up and k2 sts along edge of first 3 rows. 302 sts.
Purl 1 row.

Edging (Chart 2)
Row 1 [RS]: (LT, RT) rep to last 2 sts, LT
Row 2: *P2, k2; rep from * to last 2 sts, p2.
Row 3: *K2, p2; rep from * to last 2 sts, k2.
Rows 4-6: Work in 2x2 rib as established.
Row 7: *C2/3R, C2/3L; rep from * to last 2 sts, C2/3R.
Row 8: *K3, p3; rep from * to last 3 sts, k3.
Row 9: *P3, k3; rep from * to last 3 sts, p3.
Rows 10-12: Work in 3x3 rib as established.
Row 13: *C3/4L, C3/4R; rep from * to last 3 sts, C3/4L.
Row 14: *P4, k4; rep from * to last 4 sts, p4.
Row 15: *K4, p4; rep from * to last 4 sts, k4.
Rows 16-18: Work in 4x4 rib as established.
Bind off loosely using larger size needle. Elizabeth Zimmerman's sewn bind off is a nice alternative if you are familiar with it.

FINISHING
Weave in ends. Block.

ABOUT SAMANTHA ROSHAK
Samantha lives and plays with yarn in beautiful Seattle. You might find her taking pictures of socks in the ocean, knitting at the bus stop, or asking strangers on the street about their sweaters.

http://www.knitquest.com
KnitQuest on ravelry.com

CHART 2 - EDGING

CHART 1

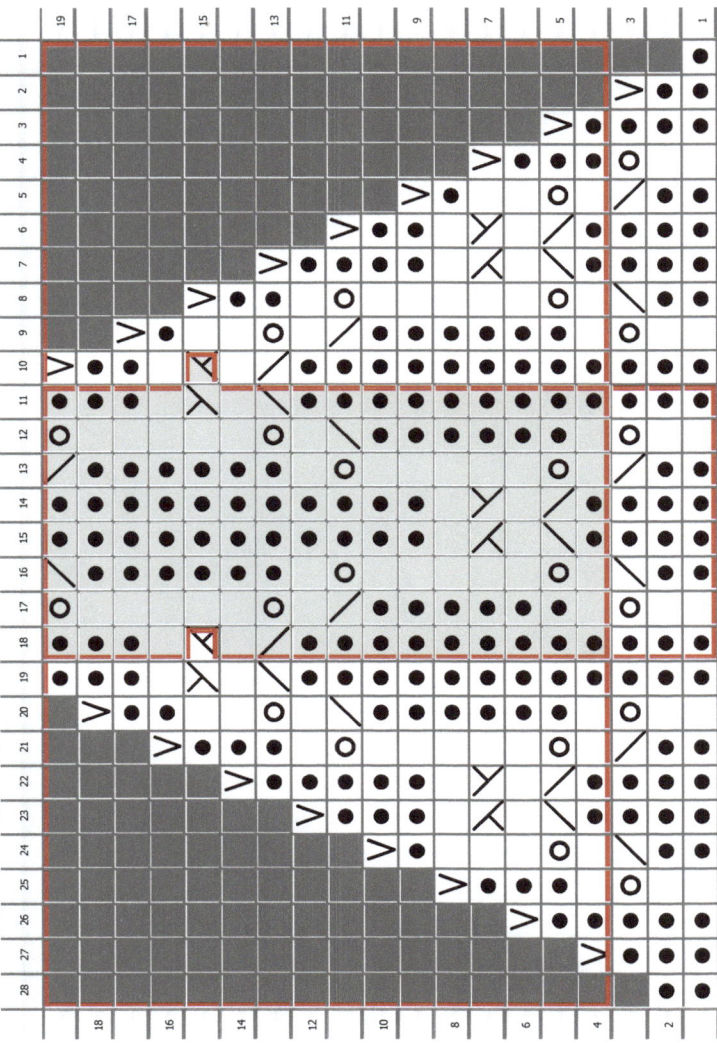

Legend:

■	**No Stitch** — RS: Placeholder - No stitch made. WS: none defined
⧅⧅	**Left Twist** — RS: sl1 to CN, hold in front. k1, k1 from CN. WS: Left Twist
⧄⧄	**Right Twist** — RS: Skip the first stitch, knit into 2nd stitch, then knit skipped stitch. Slip both stitches from needle together OR k2tog leaving sts on LH needle, then k first st again, sl both sts off needle. WS: Skip first stitch, and purl the 2nd stitch, then purl the skipped stitch. Slip both sts from needle together.
■	**No Stitch** — RS: Placeholder - No stitch made. WS: none defined
⧅⧅	**Left Twist** — RS: sl1 to CN, hold in front. k1, k1 from CN. WS: Left Twist
□	**knit** — RS: knit stitch. WS: purl stitch
•	**purl** — RS: purl stitch. WS: knit stitch
□	**knit** — RS: knit stitch. WS: purl stitch
⧄⧄⧄	**2-st cable w/inc right** — RS: sl 1 to cn, hold in back, kfb, k1 from cn. WS:
⧅⧅⧅	**2-st cable w/inc left** — RS: sl 1 to cn, hold in front, kfb, k1 from cn. WS:
⧄⧄⧄	**2-st cable w/inc right** — RS: sl 1 to cn, hold in back, kfb, k1 from cn. WS:
•	**purl** — RS: purl stitch. WS: knit stitch
⧅⧅⧅	**3-st cable w/ inc left** — RS: Sl2 to cn and hold to front, kfb, k2 from cn. WS:
⧄⧄⧄	**3-st cable w/ inc right** — RS: Sl 2 to cn and hold to back, kfb, k2 from cn. WS:
⧅⧅⧅	**3-st cable w/ inc left** — RS: Sl2 to cn and hold to front, kfb, k2 from cn. WS:
⧄	**ssk** — RS: Slip one stitch as if to knit, Slip another stitch as if to knit. Insert left-hand needle into front of these 2 stitches and knit them together. WS: Purl two stitches together in back loops, inserting needle from the left, behind and into the backs of the 2nd & 1st stitches in that order
⧅	**k2tog** — RS: Knit two stitches together as one stitch. WS: Purl 2 stitches together
○	**yo** — RS: Yarn Over. WS: Yarn Over
V	**slip** — RS: Slip stitch as if to purl, holding yarn in back. WS: Slip stitch as if to purl, holding yarn in front

FIELD OF DAISIES SHAWL

BY TABITHA'S HEART

INTERMEDIATE

My friend Daisy's wedding inspired a search for floral lace motifs. This shawl is a byproduct of that search. It features a large, open daisy pattern at the top and an ornate leaf edging. This versatile shawl can also be worn as a kerchief or scarf.

SIZE
One size

FINISHED MEASUREMENTS
Wingspan 48"/122cm
Length 18"/45.5cm

MATERIALS
Sanguine Gryphon Skinny Bugga [80% superwash merino wool, 10% cashmere, 10% nylon; 450 yd/411 m per 113g skein]; color: Southern Green Stink Bug; 1 skein

1 32-inch or longer US #8/5mm circular needle or size needed to obtain gauge
1 32-inch or longer US #9/5.5mm circular needle (or one size larger than the size needed for gauge)

Stitch markers

GAUGE
22.5 sts/24.5 rows = 4"/10cm in stockinette with smaller needle, before blocking

PATTERN NOTES
Shawl shown used every last bit of the yarn, with about 3 yards left over. When in doubt, buy extra yarn.

Kfbf: Inc 2 by knitting into front, back, front again of the same stitch.

Daisy motif is worked with double yarn overs for a very open look. When knitting back over a double yarn over on the WS, work (k1, p1) into it.

Charts show RS rows only. Work WS rows as instructed in text.

PATTERN
With smaller needle, CO 3 sts.
Row 1 [RS]: Kfb, kfbf, kfb. 7 sts.
Row 2: K2, kfb, kfbf, kfb, k2. 11 sts.
Row 3: K2, (yo, k1) 7 times, yo, k2. 19 sts.
Row 4: K2, purl to last 2 sts, k2.
Row 5: K2, yo, k2tog, yo, knit to last 4 sts, yo, ssk, yo, k2. 21 sts.
Row 6: Rep Row 4.
Row 7: K2, yo, k2tog, yo, (k3, pm) 3 times, k4, yo, ssk, yo, k2. 23 sts.
Row 8: Rep Row 4.
Row 9: K2, yo, k2tog, yo, (k to marker, M1L, sl m, k1, M1R) 3 times, k to last 4 sts, yo, ssk, yo, k2. 8 sts inc'd.
Row 10: Rep Row 4.
Row 11: K2, yo, k2tog, yo, k to first marker, M1L, sl m, k1, M1R, k to third marker, M1L, sl m, k1, M1R, k to last 4 sts, yo, ssk, yo, k2. 6 sts inc'd.
Row 12: Rep Row 4.
Rep Rows 9-12 two more times. 65 sts.

Daisy Section
Row 1 [RS]: K2, yo, k2tog, yo, k3, work Chart 1, k3, (M1L, sl m, k1, M1R, work Chart 1, k1) twice, M1L, sl m, k1, M1R, k3, work Chart 1, k3, yo, ssk, yo, k2. 8 sts inc'd.
Row 2 [WS] K2, purl to last 2 sts working (k1, p1) into each double yo, k2.
Rep Rows 1-2 until all 53 rows of Chart 1 are complete, ending with a RS row. 275 sts.
Next row [WS]: K2, purl to last 2 sts removing markers, k2.

Border
Change to larger needle. Work Rows 1-23 of Chart 2, continuing to work all WS rows as k2, purl to last 2 sts, k2.
BO all sts loosely on WS.

FINISHING
Weave in ends. Wet block shawl to dimensions or preferred size. Allow to dry thoroughly before unpinning.

ABOUT TABITHA'S HEART

Tabitha spends entirely too much time thinking about knitting. Her husband is concerned that she may be addicted. She, however, has come to the conclusion that her sanity is directly related to the amount of time she spends knitting so she has no plans to give it up.

http://www.tabithasheart.com
tabitha on ravelry.com

Legend:

■	**No Stitch** — Placeholder - No stitch made.
□	**knit** — knit stitch
⊙	**yo** — Yarn Over
╱	**k2tog** — Knit two stitches together as one stitch
╲	**ssk** — Slip one stitch as if to knit, Slip another stitch as if to knit. Insert left-hand needle into front of these 2 stitches and knit them together
⋀	**Central Double Dec** — Slip first and second stitches together as if to knit. Knit 1 stitch. Pass two slipped stitches over the knit stitch.

CHART 1

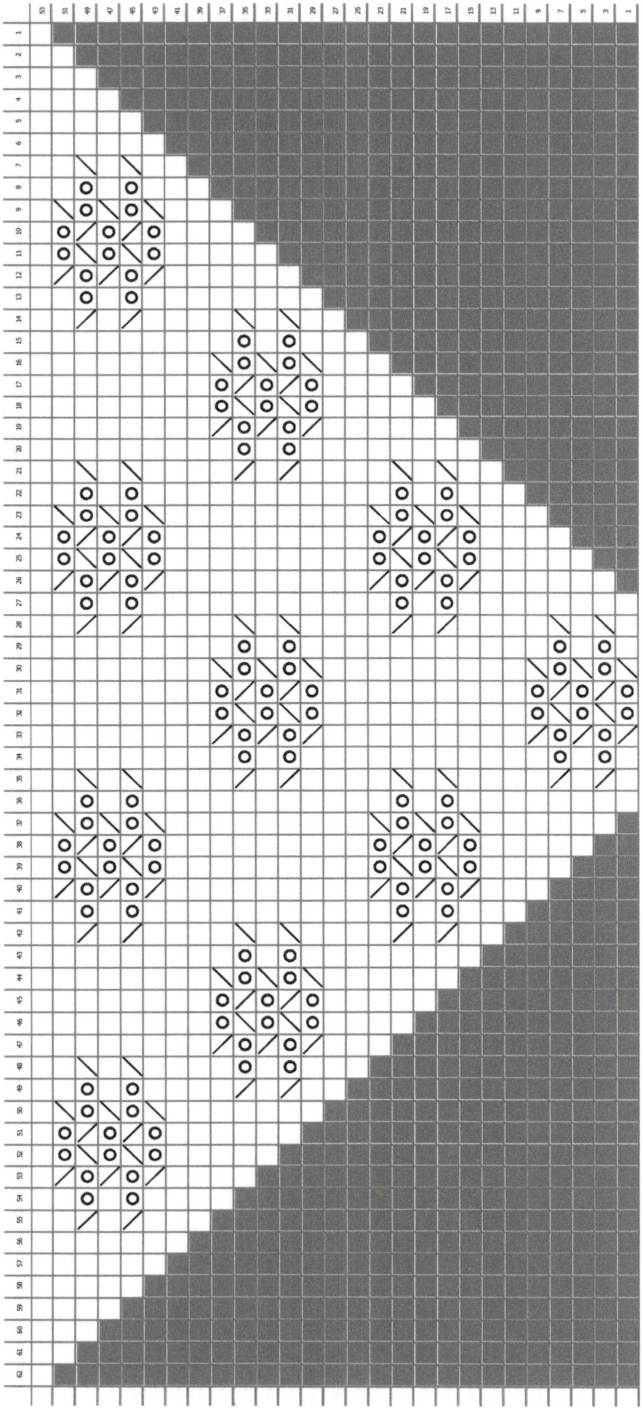

CHART 2

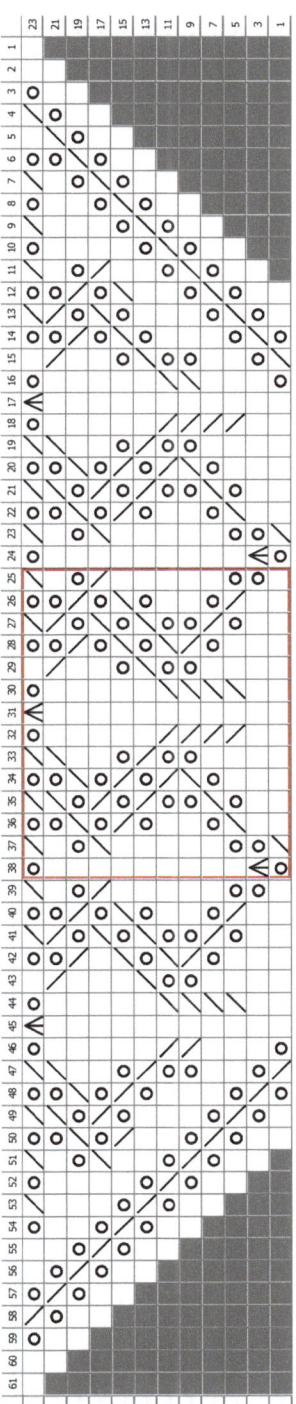

FURZELEIGH LANE SHAWLETTE

BY TERRI BATE

EXPERIENCED

Furzeleigh Lane is a beautiful little reversible shawl featuring a graceful curve to sit neatly on your shoulders or wrap snugly around your neck in scarf fashion. I designed the shawl to be knit from side to side because I find conventional patterns, which start with a couple of stitches and end with rows that go on and on and on, to be psychologically all wrong.

Furzeleigh Lane is a steep hill here in Devon, with a beautiful view of the sea at the top. (The locals pronounce it 'Fuzzleigh' Lane.) This shawl pattern likewise is all uphill whilst you're still enthusiastic. When you reach the widest part, you can pause and admire the view as it's all down hill from here! You will have mastered the lace pattern, and the rows get shorter and shorter as you get quicker and quicker.

SIZE
Small [Large]

FINISHED MEASUREMENTS
60 [68]"/152.5 [172.5]cm wide, measured along top curved edge
13.75 [15.5]"/ 35 [39.5]cm long

MATERIALS
Babylonglegs BFL Sock [100% Bluefaced Leicester wool; 464 yds per 100g skein; color Petrolhead, 1 [1] skein

1 pair US 8 [5mm] needles for larger shawl
OR 1 pair US 7 [4.5mm] needles for smaller shawl

Stitch markers

GAUGE
Gauge not critical (see Pattern Notes). The following can be used as gauge guides, if desired:
For larger shawl: 18 sts/30 rows = 4"/10cm in garter stitch
For smaller shawl: 22 sts/26 rows = 4"/10cm in garter stitch

PATTERN NOTES
Before casting on, wind your yarn into two equal-sized balls. This allows you to check how much yarn is left when you reach the center of the shawl and adjust the size if needed.

When knitting back over a double yarnover on WS, work (k1, p1) into it.

PATTERN
Cast on 2 sts.
Row 1 [WS]: Knit.
Row 2: K1, M1, k1. 3 sts.
Row 3: Knit.
Row 4: K2tog, yo, M1, k1. 4 sts.
Row 5: Knit.
Row 6: K2tog, yo, k1, yo, k1. 5 sts.
Row 7: Knit.
Row 8: K2tog, yo, k2, yo, k1. 6 sts.
Row 9: Knit.
Row 10: K2tog, yo, k3, yo, k1. 7 sts.
Row 11: K4, pm, k3.

Work Rows 1-127 of Chart 1 (see p. 43). Only RS rows are shown on this chart. Each WS row should be worked as: Knit to 4 sts before the first marker, k2tog, yo, k2, sl m, knit to end. The blue lines indicate stitch marker placement.

Work Rows 1-16 of Chart 2 once (see p. 42). Both RS and WS rows are shown on this chart and Chart 3. The first row is a WS row. For the larger shawl, work all charted stitches; for the smaller, ignore all green stitches (treat them as No Stitch squares).

Work Rows 17-28 of Chart 2 twice for smaller shawl, three times for larger shawl.
You are now almost at the center of the shawl. You should have just enough yarn left in the first ball to knit the next 8 rows. If not,

you may need to go back and remove one repeat of Rows 17-28.

Work Rows 1-16 of Chart 3 once.

Work Rows 17-28 of Chart 3 twice for smaller shawl, three times for larger shawl (or to match Chart 2 Rows 17-28, above).
Work Rows 29-45 of Chart 3 once.
Work Rows 1-129 of Chart 4. Only RS rows are shown on this chart. Each WS row should be worked as: Knit to 4 sts before the first marker, k2tog, yo, k2, sl m, knit to end.

Ending
Row 1 [WS]: Knit.
Row 2: K2tog, yo, k2, k2tog. 5 sts.
Row 3: Knit.
Row 4: K2tog, yo, k1, k2tog. 4 sts.
Row 5: Knit.
Row 6: K2tog, yo, k2tog. 3 sts.
Row 7: Knit.
Row 8: K1, k2tog. 2 sts.
Row 9: Knit.
Row 10: K2tog. 1 st.
Bind off.

FINISHING
Sew in any ends, weaving in neatly. Wash gently in warm suds, rinse and remove as much water as possible before pinning out on blocking board. Leave flat to dry.

ABOUT TERRI BATE
Terri Bate works as an NHS midwife on Dartmoor in Devon, in the foot of England. In her spare time, she runs an annual fiber retreat at Samhain/Hallowe'en, organizes a teashop knitting and spinning club and is a committee member of the Weavers', Spinners', Dyers' Guild in Devon. She delights in walking her dog across the moors (with her drop spindle), or snuggling in front of the fire with a good book (and her knitting).

http://knitknackpaddywack.blogspot.com
tutleymutley on ravelry.com

CHART

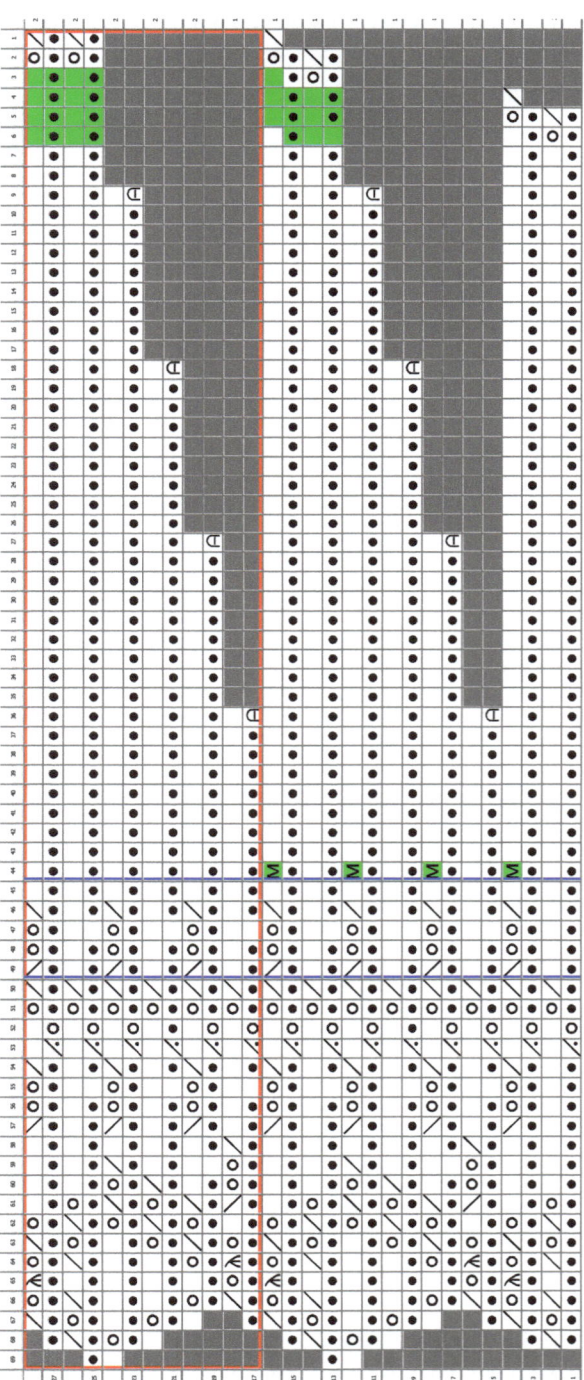

CHART 1

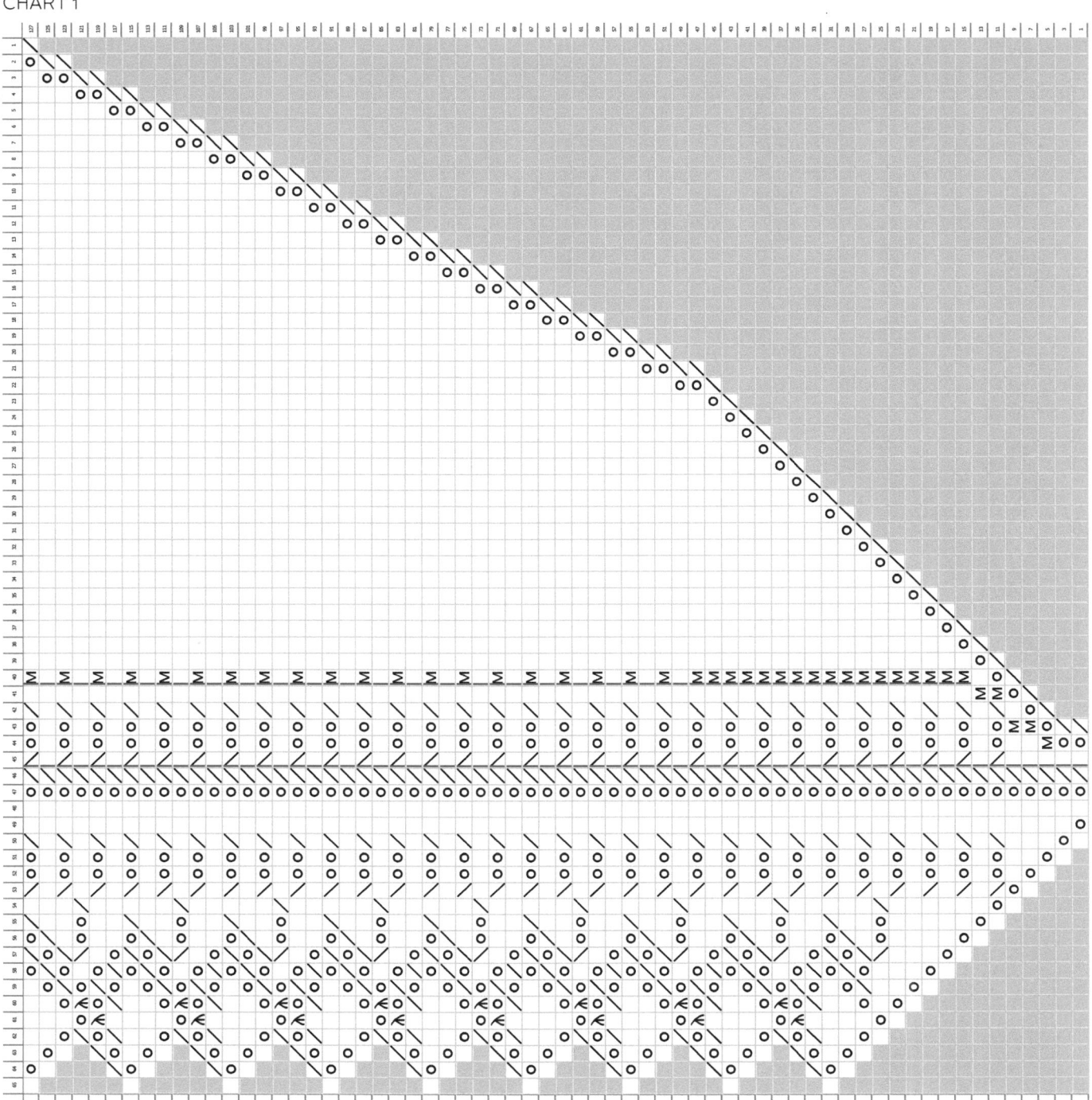

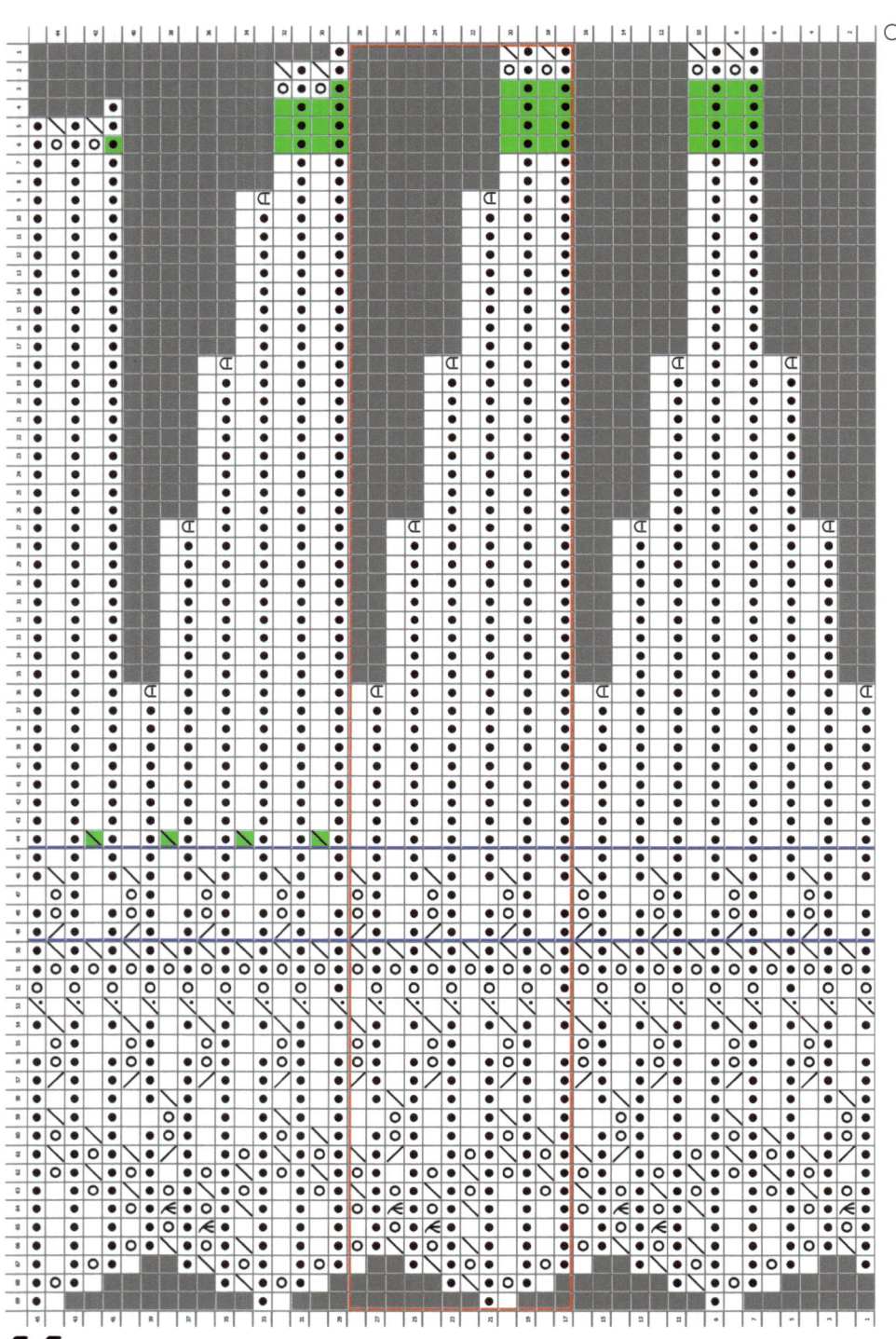

CHART 4

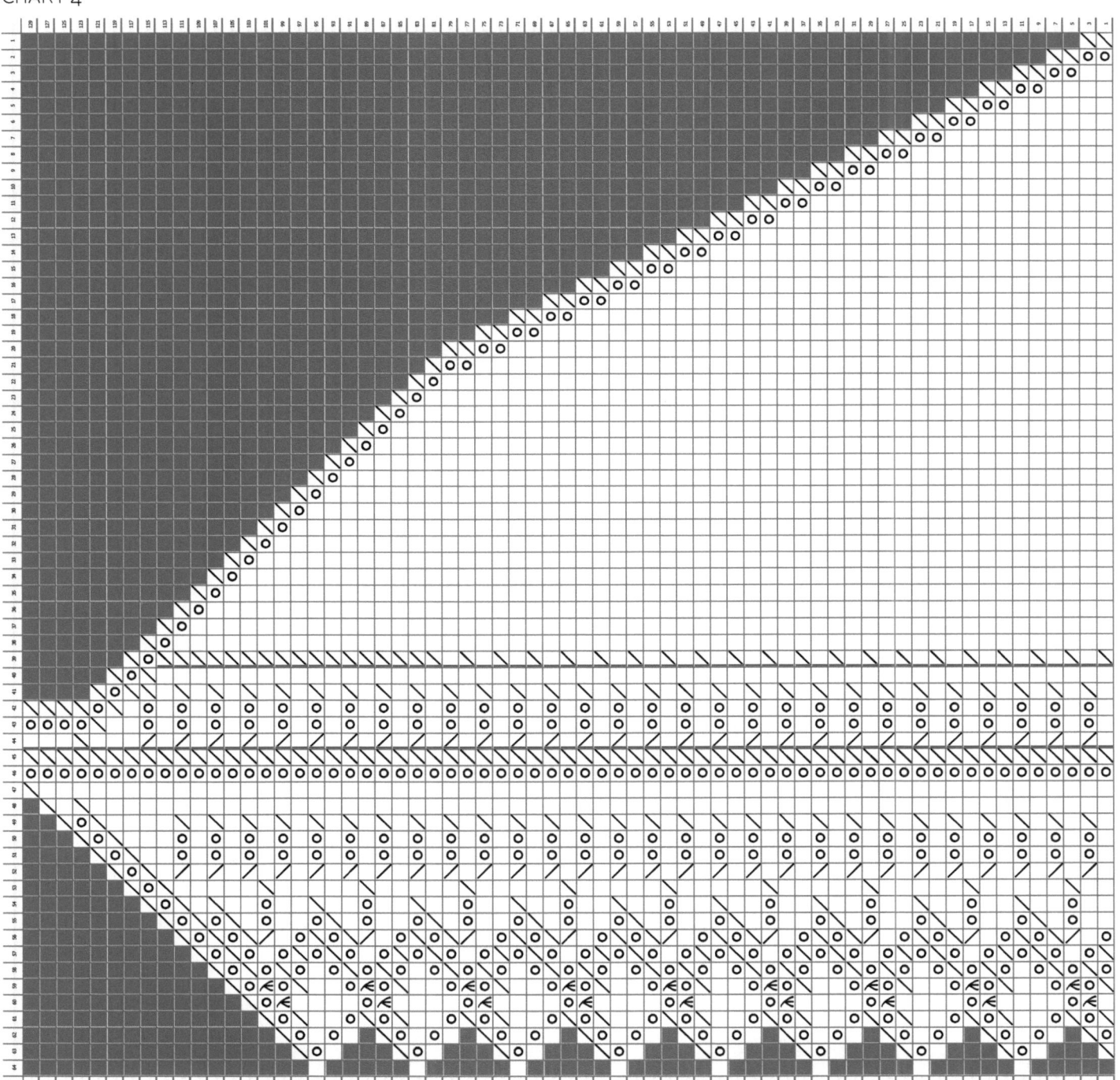

GEOMETRY WRAP
BY THERESSA SILVER

EASY

With multiple ways to wear it, Geometry combines the all-wrapped-up cozy feeling of a shawl with the easy-to-wear simplicity of a vest. The front pieces can be worn across the body and either buttoned along their bottom edges (as shown) or buttoned along their sides for a more tailored look. The fronts can also come straight over the shoulders and be buttoned along their sides to create an open vest. The right angles and curves that give this wrap its name also allow for easy, one-piece construction.

SIZE
S/M [L/XL, 2X/3X]
Measure across the wearer's back at the level of the armpits. Use this measurement to determine which size to make, rounding up to allow for wearing ease. The front sections of the wrap can be altered to accommodate larger or smaller busts without changing the fit across the back.

FINISHED MEASUREMENTS
Across back: 15.5 [18, 20.5]"/39.5 [45.5, 52]cm

MATERIALS
Three Irish Girls Galenas Merino [100% merino wool; 220yd/200m per 100g skein]; color: Cameron; 4 [4, 5] skeins

1 24 inch US #9/5.5mm circular needle
1 set US #9/5.5mm double-point needles (optional)

Stitch holders
Stitch markers
10 or 12 3/4" [19mm] buttons

GAUGE
18 sts/28 rows = 4"/10cm in stockinette

PATTERN NOTES
This wrap is knit from the center of the back outwards. It is started in the round on a circular needle, using the magic loop method. Stitch counters are used to break up the work into 3 sections. If you prefer to start on double pointed needles, cast onto 3 needles. When the dpns get too full, switch to the circular needle. After the center back is knit in the round, the 3 sections are divided and worked separately back-and-forth to form the lower back and the two front pieces.

PATTERN
Back
Cast on 7 sts and join to work in the round.
Rnd 1: K2, pm, k2, pm, k3, pm.
Rnd 2: (K1, m1, k1) 3 times, m1, k1. 3-3-5 sts in each section.
Rnd 3 and all odd-numbered rnds: Knit.
Rnd 4: *(K1, m1) twice, k1; rep from * once, (k1, m1) 4 times, k1. 5-5-9 sts.
Rnd 6: *K1, m1, k2tog, k1, m1, k1, sl m; rep from * once, k1, m1, k2, k2tog, k3, m1, k1. 6-6-10 sts.
Rnds 8 and 10: *K1, m1, k to last st before marker, m1, k1, sl m; rep from * to end. 10-10-14 sts.
Rnd 12: *K1, m1, k1 to last st before m, m1, k1, sl m; rep from * once, k1, m1, (kfb) 5 times, k2, (kfb) 5 times, m1, k1. 12-12-26 sts.
Rnds 14, 16, 18: Rep Rnd 8. 18-18-32 sts.
Rnd 20: *K1, m1, k to last st before m, m1, k1, sl m; rep from * once, k1, m1, (kfb) twice, (k1, kfb, kfb) 4 times, k2, (kfb, kfb, k1) 4 times, (kfb) twice, m1, k1. 20-20-54 sts.
Rnds 22, 24, 26: Rep Rnd 8. 26-26-60 sts.
Rnd 28: *K1, m1, k to last st before m, m1, k1, sl m; rep from * once, k1, m1, k2, (k3, kfb) 6 times, k6, (kfb, k3) 6 times, k2, m1, k1. 28-28-74 sts.
Rnds 30, 32, 34: Rep Rnd 8. 34-34-80 sts.
Rnd 36: *K1, m1, k to last st before m, m1, k1, sl m; rep from * once, k1, m1, (k6, kfb) 5 times, k8, (kfb, k6) 5 times, m1, k1. 36-36-92 sts.
Rnds 38, 40, 42: Rep Rnd 8. 42-42-98 sts.
Rnd 44: *K1, m1, k to last st before m, m1, k1, sl m; rep from * once, k1, m1, (k8, kfb) 5 times, k6, (kfb, k8) 5 times, m1, k1. 44-44-110 sts.

Size S/M, skip to Lower Back, below.

Sizes L/1X and 2X/3X:
Rnds 46, 48, 50: Rep Rnd 8. 50-50-116 sts.
Rnd 52: *K1, m1, k to last st before m, m1, k1, sl m; rep from * once, k1, m1, (k12, kfb) 4 times, k10, (kfb, k12) 4 times, m1, k1. 52-52-126 sts.

Size L/1X, skip to Lower Back, below.

Size 2X/3X only:
Rnds 54, 56, 58: Rep Rnd 8. 58-58-132 sts.
Rnd 60: *K1, m1, k to last st before m, m1, k1, sl m; rep from * once, k1, m1 (k9, kfb) 6 times, k10, (kfb, k9) 6 times, m1, k1. 60-60-146 sts.

Lower Back
Knit 1 rnd.
Place the stitches from the first two sections (those with the smaller number of sts) onto separate holders. The remaining 110 [126, 146] sts will be worked back-and-forth from now on.
Row 1 [WS]: K4, *p2, k2; rep from * to last 2 sts, k2.
Row 2 [RS]: K4, *k2, p2; rep from * to last 2 sts, p2.
Rep Rows 1-2 for 2.5"/6.5cm, ending with a RS row.
Next row [WS]: K4, p7 [10, 9], M1P, *p8 [9, 8], M1P; rep from * to last 11 [13, 13] sts, p7 [9, 9], k4. 122 [138, 162] sts.
Next row: Knit.
Next row: K4, purl to last 4 sts, k4.
Rep the last 2 rows until work measures 9"/23cm from bottom of ribbing, ending with a WS row.

Bottom edging
Row 1 [RS]: K4, *p2, k2; rep from * to last 2 sts, k2.
Row 2: K6, *p1, yo, p1, k2; rep from * to last 4 sts, k4.
Row 3: K4, p2, *k3, p2; rep from * to last 4 sts, k4.
Row 4: K6, *p3, k2; rep from * to last 4 sts, k4.
Row 5: K4, p2, *k3, pass first knit st over the next two and off RH needle, p2; rep from * to last 4 sts, k4.
Row 6: K6, *p2, k2; rep from * to last 4 sts, k4.
Bind off in pattern.

Left Upper Back and Front
Transfer the 44 [52, 60] held sts from the first section to needle and join yarn with RS facing.
Row 1 [RS]: K3, p2, k to last 5 sts, p2, k3.
Row 2: K1, p1, yo, p1, k2, purl to last 5 sts, k2, p1, yo, p1, k1.
Row 3: K4, p2, k to last 6 sts, p2, k4.
Row 4: K1, p3, k2, purl to last 6 sts, k2, p3, k1.
Row 5: K1, k3, pass first knit st over the next two and off RH needle, p2, k to last 6 sts, p2, k3, pass first knit st over the next two and off RH needle, k1.
Rep Rows 2-5 until piece is 2"/5cm shorter than required finished length, ending with Row 5. This piece needs to be long enough to go over the shoulder, curve over the bust and overlap the lower back at the underarm (see photo). The total length will depend on your height, bust size, and desired fit.

Bottom edging
Row 1 [WS]: K1, p1, yo, p1, k2, purl to last 5 sts, k2, p1, yo, p1, k1.
Row 2: K4, p2, k to last 6 sts, p2, k4.
Row 3: K1, p3, k2, purl to last 6 sts, k2, p3, k1.
Row 4: K1, k3, pass first knit st over the next two and off RH needle, *p2, k2; rep from * to last 6 sts, p2, k3, pass first knit st over the next two and off RH needle, k1.
Row 5: K1, *p1, yo, p1, k2; rep from * to last 3 sts, p1, yo, p1, k1.
Row 6: K4, *p2, k3; rep from * to 6 sts, p2, k4.
Row 7: K1, *p3, k2; rep from * to last 4 sts, p3, k1.
Row 8: K1, *k3, pass first knit st over the next two and off RH needle, p2; rep from * to last 4 sts, k3, pass first knit st over the next two and off RH needle, k1.
Row 9: K1, *p2, k2; rep from * to last 3 sts, p2, k1.
Bind off in pattern.

Right Upper Back and Front
Work same as Left side.

FINISHING
Weave in ends. Block. Attach buttons to the lower back button bands to correspond with the yarn overs along the bottom and sides of the front pieces, allowing one button for every third hole.

ABOUT THERESSA SILVER
Theressa is inspired by the endless flexibility and shape-ability of knit fabric to test the limits and create the unexpected. She lives in Oregon with her husband, son, four cats, and a dog; all of whom participate one way or another in the knitting process.

http://www.argentgal.com
argentgal on ravelry.com

ACKNOWLEDGMENTS

Thank you to the designers who created such beautiful work for the book. Our biggest thanks to photographer Robert Gladys, makeup artist Elle Gemma, and to our models Arabella Proffer, Rachel Harner, Susan Prahst and Terra Incognita, as well as to Abra Forman, whose considerable talents helped bring the project together in its early stages. Sarah Jo Burch helped keep things running so Abra and Shannon could get things done, and MJ Kim did a massive amount of organizational work before we handed everything off to the talented technical editor, Alexandra Virgiel. Elizabeth Green Musselman came late to the team but helped enormously with wrapping up loose ends.

The book wouldn't be nearly as beautiful without the yarns contributed by the companies below.

We'd also like to thank the generous patrons whose Kickstarter support helped make this book series possible.

YARNS FEATURED IN THIS BOOK:

Waterloo Wools	(http://www.waterloowools.com)
Lisa Souza	(http://www.lisaknit.com)
Sanguine Gryphon	has split into two companies since this book was commissioned: (http://verdantgryphon.com) and (http://cephalopodyarns.com)
Karabella Yarns	(http://www.karabellayarns.com)
Pigeonroof Studios	(http://www.etsy.com/shop/pigeonroofstudios)
A Verb for Keeping Warm	(http://www.averbforkeepingwarm.com)
Blue Moon Fiber Arts	(http://www.bluemoonfiberarts.com)
Babylonglegs	(http://babylonglegs.bigcartel.com)
Three Irish Girls	(http://www.threeirishgirls.com)

ABOUT COOPERATIVE PRESS

partners in publishing

Cooperative Press (formerly anezka media) was founded in 2007 by Shannon Okey, a voracious reader as well as writer and editor, who had been doing freelance acquisitions work, introducing authors with projects she believed in to editors at various publishers.

Although working with traditional publishers can be very rewarding, there are some books that fly under their radar. They're too avant-garde, or the marketing department doesn't know how to sell them, or they don't think they'll sell 50,000 copies in a year.

5,000 or 50,000. Does the book matter to that 5,000? Then it should be published.

In 2009, Cooperative Press changed its named to reflect the relationships we have developed with authors working on books. We work together to put out the best quality books we can, and share in the proceeds accordingly.

Thank you for supporting independent publishers and authors.

We're on Ravelry as CooperativePress. Please join our low-volume mailing list and check out our other books at...

HTTP://WWW.COOPERATIVEPRESS.COM

ABOUT FRESH DESIGNS

Shannon Okey wanted to do something to showcase emerging design talent after she left the editorship of a UK print knitting magazine; Fresh Designs is the result. A partnership between talented designers and primarily small/indie yarn companies (all of whom are thanked on the previous page — please help support these remarkable companies when you next shop for yarn), the first 10 Fresh Designs books have also broken the mold for designer compensation. Each time you purchase a Fresh Designs book or pattern, the designers receive a royalty share. We hope you'll enjoy meeting the designers in these pages, and that you'll check out the other books in the Fresh Designs series.

ABBREVIATIONS

alt	alternate
approx	approximately
beg	begin/beginning
BO	bind off
CC	contrasting color
cn	cable needle
CO	cast on
dec	decrease(s)/decreasing
dpn	double pointed needle
est	established
foll	follows/following
inc	increase(s)/increasing
k	knit
k2tog	knit 2 together
kfb	knit into the front and back of the same stitch
kwise	knitwise
LH	left hand
m1	make 1 stitch
M1L	make 1 left
M1P	make 1 purl
M1R	make 1 right
MC	main color
p	purl
patt	pattern
pm	place marker
p2tog	purl 2 together
psso	pass slipped st over
pwise	purlwise
rem	remain/remaining
rep(s)	repeat(s)
RH	right hand
rnd(s)	round(s)
RS	right side
sl	slip
ssk	slip, slip, knit these 2 sts together
tbl	through the back loop
tog	together
WS	wrong side
wyib	with yarn in back
wyif	with yarn in front
yo	yarn over

53